THE RELIGION
OF
BENJAMIN FRANKLIN

BENJAMIN FRANKLIN

Reproduction of portrait given by Dr. Franklin to Richard Oswald after the preliminary articles of peace were signed in 1782.

THE RELIGION OF BENJAMIN FRANKLIN

BY

JAMES MADISON STIFLER

D. APPLETON AND COMPANY
NEW YORK :: 1925 :: LONDON

CBPac

96921

COPYRIGHT, 1925, BY
D. APPLETON AND COMPANY

PREFACE

This volume seems to me an interesting and valuable addition to the literature on Benjamin Franklin. So far as I know, it is the first work on the subject available for the general reader, and, springing from first-hand investigation of original material, it bears the marks of patient research and impresses the reader as being a fair and trustworthy treatment of the subject. Franklin is one of the most lovable and useful figures in the early history of America. Well known though he has been through his practical inventions, his religious life and thought have been generally misunderstood. This volume, by supplementing the fragmentary references in the Autobiography with the ampler and more revealing material in the letters, corrects many popular misapprehensions and deserves the careful consideration of all who are interested in the religious origins of America.

HARRY EMERSON FOSDICK.

FOREWORD

The writer of the following pages is not a historian. One who takes up this book thinking to find a specimen of the work of the professional will be disappointed. It was written for pure pleasure in the hours stolen from the crowded days of a large and active parish. If it gives to any reader a shadow of the quiet delight that the composition of it has produced, it has fulfilled its mission.

A word should be said about the reason for its undertaking. As a graduate of the university that Benjamin Franklin founded, and saturated with traditions about him, I had more than ordinary interest in his personality. There formed gradually in my mind a wonder as to what sort of religion he might have had. The casual friend to whom the religion of Benjamin Franklin was mentioned generally replied that he didn't know that Franklin had any religion. I could not believe, however, that the autobiography with its frequent references to moral standards and expressions of

vii

confidence in God could grow from a wholly irreligious soil.

About this time I had the good fortune to be introduced to a private library so rich in Franklin material that I could not resist the inclination to give more time to pursue my question as to what sort of religion, if any, this great national character had.

If the result has any merit it is largely due to the unimaginable wealth of material to which I have had access and to the friendly guidance and assistance of Mr. W. S. Mason in whose library most of the work has been done.

I am greatly indebted also to Mr. Theodore W. Koch, librarian at Northwestern University, and to Mr. George Simpson Eddy of New York, who have read the manuscript and made suggestions that have added to the value of the work.

If the book has any claim to attention it is due to the fact that it is the first attempt to deal at any length with this aspect of Franklin's character and also that it has had the advantage of practically all known and much hitherto little known and unpublished material.

J. M. S.

ILLUSTRATIONS

THE RELIGION OF
BENJAMIN FRANKLIN

THE RELIGION OF BENJAMIN FRANKLIN

WE stand in need of a liberal spirit and a considerable share of modesty when we attempt
an appraisal of the spiritual state of a man who
has been dead for more than a century. The task
is complicated when that hundred years has been
marked by such fundamental changes in spiritual
conceptions as has this last. If our subject were
an ecclesiastic or a theologian the task would apparently be easier; apparently only, because we
have learned to know the very great difference between a man's religion, which is his actual experience of spiritual things, and his theology, which
is his effort to account for his experience.
So we say it would have appeared to be
easier. We could somewhat easily classify his
theology, but we might not then be quite sure that
we had the real description of what he himself
actually believed and practiced.

Without being dogmatic, we ought to be able
to arrive at a fairly close estimate of Franklin's

religion because he has left us such an endless array of evidence. He was a letter writer of the first rank both in quantity, and in the freedom and charm with which he expressed himself. Franklin is a bright exception to the rule that real wisdom does not go with a loquacious disposition. He was both wise and talkative. Most of his letters were not written with one eye on the publisher, but bear the marks of genuine simplicity and directness of personal intent. This is much less true, of course, with regard to the autobiography which was confessedly written to be read. Between the letters and the autobiography we have a most unusual personal record.

Another cause for hesitation in such an inquiry is that there is such an abysmal gulf between what one man and another call religion.

Let us assume, therefore, that by that term we mean a man's experience of God and his manner of conduct flowing therefrom. This, of course, sounds as if we were confusing religion and ethics, but we are not, for a man's religion is the foundation of his ethical standard, and his ethical conduct is the signpost of his actual beliefs.

We must try to play fair with our subject, too, in the matter of perspective. If we start to compare him with religious men of our own time or to compare his ideas with the conceptions of religion in our day we are unfair to him, just as we are often unfair to those New Englanders who burned witches at the stake. They did it, it is true, but they were slower to begin and quicker to stop than their contemporaries across the water and the total number of their witch-burnings was infinitesimal in comparison with other groups of their day. Their conduct in the witch-burning era was distinctly humanitarian. Franklin must be looked at and judged by the men and religion of his own lifetime.

The inquiry has a certain practical value because Franklin was the spring from which flowed one of the most formative influences in our national character. It is of real value to endeavor to find out the spiritual nature from which such an influence came. The idea has gained ground among Americans that Franklin was not at all religious. But he was certainly not a Gallio. He never could be classed among these amiable modern pagans, who seldom if ever entertain any thought of God and scarce know what one is talking about when God is mentioned. He was not dissociated from the religious life of his own day. Indeed we shall see he had a fairly active share in it. What we want to find out is just how far that association went.

He certainly was not a pagan, and with equal assurance he was not an orthodox Christian in his own time. Just where between those extremes was he?

Benjamin Franklin came from a religious family. His ancestors were among those that embraced the reformed faith in England. They were of the sturdy stock that stood by their convictions through the days of Bloody Mary. The story that he tells of his great-great-grandfather and the Bible that was held by tapes under the lid of the joint stool is illuminating. When the Bible was to be read one child stood guard at the door. If the officers were seen coming, the stool was turned down and the sin of Bible reading concealed. There is considerable spiritual fiber in human beings like that, and it had not run out when their descendants came to New England.

The exponents of some modern schools of heredity would probably say that it was very natural that Franklin should have had an interest in spiritual things, even though that interest did not flow in orthodox channels, which it certainly did not. He not only came from a line of religiously disposed ancestors but his father actually intended to devote Benjamin to the ministry, as a tithe of his children. His father, Josiah, with his wife and three children came to New England about 1682. Four children were born of this wife, and a second wife, Abiah Folger, bore him ten more, of whom Benjamin was the ninth child and the youngest son.

On the very day of his birth Josiah Franklin took the infant Benjamin across the street to the old South Church and had him baptized. So Benjamin Franklin was started off in life in a highly orthodox fashion destined for the Christian ministry. In carrying out this intention the boy was very early sent to school, which meant a "pay" school as there were no others. But Josiah's family was large, and his occupation as tallow-chandler and soap-boiler was not very remunerative so when Benjamin was about ten years old he was taken from his books and set to helping his father about the shop.

His father had an educational ideal, however, and evidently clung to it tenaciously. Though he could not afford to keep a child in school he did all that he could to encourage and stimulate his children's mental development. Franklin relates that one thing that his father did in this direction was to invite as often as he could some sensible friend or neighbor to the family table and designedly start some ingenious or useful topic for discussion. This was not a bad way to develop young minds, when food was cheap and tuition high.

Though he could not go to school, the boy did develop a taste for books. His first recorded purchase was John Bunyan's works in a series of little volumes. It is an interesting speculation as to what sort of a man Benjamin Franklin might have become if he had had in those early years a wise and sympathetic guide for his exceptional mind. Without a doubt, some of the more unworthy phases of his youth with their resultant effects on his character would have been different. But the perfect teacher is rare and Franklin had to battle his own way out through the briars and hedges of uncongenial occupation and a good deal of unsympathetic opposition.

His bookish inclination finally made it evident that he would not make a first-class soap-boiler, so his father, who seems a fairly wise and kindly intentioned man, took Benjamin from the tallow shop and apprenticed him to his older brother, James, who was a printer. As he grew a little older his inquiring mind and normal resentment towards repressing surroundings bore its natural fruit. He developed a taste for the writings of skeptics and confesses that by the time he was sixteen he was a "staunch doubter" and, whenever possible, avoided attendance in the family pew.

The peculiar set of Franklin's mind, the disposition to clear and balanced thinking, as we might expect, showed itself very early. He tells in the *Autobiography* that about this period, in his late "teens," there fell into his hands some books which were evidently written by orthodox churchmen in opposition to Deism. He says that the arguments of the Deists that were put up to be refuted seemed to him so much superior to the refutation that he became in his own mind a staunch Deist. This storm and stress period continued until he was about nineteen and culminated while he was in London in his writing a pamphlet designed to refute the fundamental tenets of Christianity as he knew them. The pamphlet was entitled "A Dissertation on Liberty and Necessity, Pleasure and Pain."

Tradition has caught hold of his writing of this pamphlet and given rise to the vague impression which the average person has that Benjamin Franklin was an antireligious man.

The entire truth of this epoch in his youthful thinking and writing was about this: He did write such a pamphlet but very soon afterward felt that he could not stand by it, as he puts it,

"I began to suspect that this doctrine, though it might be true, was not very useful . . . and I doubted whether some error had not insinuated itself unperceived into my argument."

The natural swing of a penetrating mind's reaction to such a venture was, as might have been expected, a motion in the opposite direction toward orthodoxy. The next thing that he wrote was a pamphlet arguing for the validity of prayer. Not only did he do this, but at the same time he destroyed all the copies of the "Dissertation" that he could recall.

Since the publication of this pamphlet has had a strong hold on the imagination of so many people, perhaps it may be interesting to have Franklin's own story of it more in detail. The publication of the pamphlet was made a subject of some inquiry when Franklin was seventy-three years old.

Benjamin Vaughan, in a letter dated July 30, 1779, asked Franklin: "Pray did you write a piece on Liberty and Necessity,[1] printed for Shackford or Shuckurgh in 1729 or 1739, with a dedication to truth: the burthen of the piece being

---

[1] The writer has examined a copy of this pamphlet, and quite agrees with Smyth, who says that it has no merit and that he could not reprint it after Franklin had suppressed it.

that the mind was acted upon by ideas, as the body was by matter; and an analysis of the mind's operations was there given out? The piece was short." Priestley made a similar inquiry (May 8, 1779): "I have just seen but have had no opportunity to read, a pamphlet in favor of the doctrine of Necessity printed, I think, in 1729, and dedicated to *Truth*. Is this the tract you told me you wrote, and could not procure me a copy of? I cannot help being desirous of knowing this circumstance." To which Franklin replied: "I did not write the pamphlet you mention. I know nothing of it. . . . I suppose it is the same, concerning which Dr. Priestley formerly asked me the same question. That for which he took it was entitled, *A Dissertation on Liberty and Necessity, Pleasure and Pain,* with these lines in the title page:

Whatever is, is right, But purblind Man
Sees but a part o' the Chain, the nearest Link,
His Eye not carrying to that equal Beam,
That poises all above.

DRYDEN.
London, Printed MDCCXXV

"It was addressed to Mr. J. R., that is, James Ralph, then a youth of about my age, and my intimate friend; afterwards a political writer and historian. The purport of it was to prove the doctrine of fate, from the supposed attributes of God; in some such manner as this: that in erecting and governing the world, as he was infinitely wise, he knew what would be best; infinitely good, he must be disposed, and infinitely powerful, he must be able to execute it: consequently all is right. There were only an hundred copies printed, of which I gave a few to friends, and afterwards disliking the piece, as conceiving it might have an ill tendency, I burnt the rest, except one copy, the margin of which was filled with manuscript notes by Lyons, author of *The Infallibility of Human Judgment,* who was at that time another of my acquaintances in London. I was not nineteen years of age when it was written. In 1730, I wrote a piece on the other side of the question, which began with laying for its foundation this fact: 'That almost all men in all ages and countries have at times made use of prayer.' Thence I reasoned, that if all things are ordained, prayer must among the rest be ordained. But as prayer can produce no change in things that are ordained, praying must be useless and an absurdity. God would therefore not ordain praying if everything else was ordained. But praying exists, therefore all things are not ordained, etc. This pamphlet was never printed, and the manuscript has been long lost. The great uncertainty I found in metaphysical reasonings disgusted me, and I quitted that kind of reading and study for others more satisfactory."

The next evidence of a religious expression in Franklin's life comes at the age of twenty-two when he composed a small liturgy or form of prayer for his own private use, entitled *Articles of Belief and Acts of Religion.*

The little book is in Franklin's own handwriting, most carefully and neatly done.

The book begins with a formal statement of his belief in the character of God, and the description of that character. Should the limits of this inquiry permit, it would be interesting to quote from it at length. Then follows an invocation, resembling in style some of the Psalms of David:

O Creator, O Father! I believe that thou art Good, and that thou art *pleas'd with the pleasure* of thy children. Praised be thy name for ever!

By thy Power hast thou made the glorious Sun, with his attending Worlds; from the energy of thy mighty Will, they first received motion; and by thy wisdom hast thou prescribed the wondrous laws, by which they move. Praised be thy name for ever!

By thy wisdom hast thou formed all things. Thou hast created man, bestowing life and reason, and placed him in dignity superior to thy other earthly creatures. Praised be thy name for ever!

These and similar sentences are to be solemnly pronounced, and the worshiper was next to read a passage from Ray's *Wisdom of God in the Creation*, or other books that are mentioned, then was to be sung Milton's hymn to the Creator, beginning:

"These are thy glorious works, Parent of good!
Almighty, thine this universal frame."

Then followed a litany from which we must quote the prelude at length, as it reveals much of the depth of this young man's mature thought:

Inasmuch as by reason of our ignorance we cannot be certain that many things, which we often hear mentioned in the petitions of men to the Deity, would prove real goods, if they were in our possession, and as I have reason to hope and believe that the goodness of my Heavenly Father will not withhold from me a suitable share of temporal blessings, if by a virtuous and holy life I conciliate his favor and kindness, therefore I presume not to ask such things, but rather humbly and with a sincere heart, express my earnest desires that he would graciously assist my continual endeavors and resolutions of eschewing vice and embracing virtue; which kind of supplications will *at least be thus far beneficial, as they remind me* in a solemn manner of my extensive duty.

The litany followed, from which we read as samples of what the young Franklin thought he ought to pray:

That I may be preserved from atheism and infidelity, impiety and profaneness, and, in my addresses to Thee, carefully avoid irreverence and ostentation, formality and odious hypocrisy— Help me, O Father!

That I may to those above me be dutiful, humble, and submissive; avoiding pride, disrespect, and contumacy—Help me, O Father!

That I may to those below me be gracious, condescending, and forgiving, using clemency, protecting *innocent distress*, avoiding cruelty, harshness, and oppression, insolence, and unreasonable severity—Help me, O Father!

This is the tenor of all the prayers, of which there are a good many.

There is every reason for belief that Franklin made regular use of his liturgy for a considerable period after its composition. Now prayer is probably the highest act of religion of which men are capable. A man who finds himself out of sympathy with organized religion as he finds it about him, and has enough religious vitality to develop a prayer scheme of his own, gives evidence of far more than ordinary religious disposition.

Back of all expressions of religion, of whatever sort they may be, lies a sense of God, and this Franklin unquestionably had throughout his whole life. His very struggles over Deism and Theism and his various encounters with preachers, churches, and evangelists, some of which we shall consider, never beclouded his fixed confidence in God. On the contrary, they bespeak a deep feeling for the existence and reality of the Deity and his meaning in man's life.

It is interesting to observe the look of surprise that one often arouses when the fact is stated that Benjamin Franklin was a good deal of a churchgoer. Yet anything else would have been more surprising in view of his early training and his very active interest in matters of religious belief. Had the churches in Philadelphia been of a more liberal disposition the probability is that Franklin would have been more devoted. It is equally probable that had they met the full approval of his vigorous and liberal thinking most of the other worshipers would have left. Franklin was a full generation ahead of his age, and his efforts to be at home in the churches in Philadelphia are evidence of the fact. Yet he went to church, wherever he could stand it. Later in life he was evidently a sermon taster of considerable ability though he was generally present as a supporter and spectator rather than a hearty coöperator.

Of his earlier experiences at churchgoing in Philadelphia he writes:

Tho' I seldom attended any public worship, I had still an opinion of its propriety, and of its utility when rightly conducted, and I regularly paid my annual subscription for the support of the only Presbyterian minister or meeting we had in Philadelphia. He us'd to visit me sometimes as a friend, and admonish me to attend his administrations, and I was now and then prevail'd on to do so, once for five Sundays successively. [One can see the twinkle in his eyes as he wrote that phrase.] Had he been in my opinion a good preacher, perhaps I might have continued, notwithstanding the occasion I had for the Sunday's leisure in my course of study.

It might be profitable for preachers to read the incident that finally closed Franklin's attendance on preaching at that church. It was this:

At length he took for his text, "Finally, brethren, whatsoever things are true, honest, just, pure, lovely or of good report, if there be any virtue, or any praise think on these things." And I imagin'd, in a sermon on such a text, we could not miss of having some morality. But he confin'd himself to five points only, as meant by the apostle, viz.:

1. Keeping holy the Sabbath day
2. Being diligent in reading the holy Scriptures
3. Attending duly the public worship
4. Partaking of the Sacrament
5. Paying a due respect to God's ministers

These might be all good things; but, as they were not the kind of good things that I expected from that text, I despaired of ever meeting with them from any other, was disgusted, and attended his preaching no more.

But his churchgoing habits could not be wholly eradicated, even by such bizarre exegesis as had caused his great disgust. In 1734, when he was twenty-eight years old, there appeared in Philadelphia a young Presbyterian preacher named Hemphill. He had a good voice and apparently spoke extempore, and Franklin writes that he, among many others, became one of his regular hearers— "His sermons pleasing me, as they had little of the dogmatical kind, but inculcated strongly the practice of virtue, or what in the religious style are called good works."

This very thing, however, caused trouble with the other and more orthodox hearers, and the young man was held for heresy. Franklin wrote some pamphlets for him. Curiously enough, this man who was so easily displeased with bad exegesis, stood by Hemphill even when it was proved that at least one of his sermons was clear plagiarism, and when he confessed to Franklin that his good preaching was due mostly to a good

memory. Franklin says that he "Rather ap-
prov'd his giving us good sermons compos'd by
others, than bad ones of his own manufacture,
tho' the latter was the practice of our common
teachers." But the young memorizer was driven
from his pulpit.

Franklin then quitted his pew, but continued
his subscription for many years. However, when
he discontinued his attendance on preaching that
seemed to him unworthy, it did not mean that
he dropped all thoughts of religion. On the contrary, one who reads the letters written during
his thirties will discover that he gave much thought
to the very essence of religion, the fruits of the
spirit. This was at the time when he was actively
engaged in laying the foundations of his fortune,
a time when many men give apparently little
thought to religious matters. In the letters of
this period, as in those that followed in later
years, it is apparent that Franklin had a very
clear conviction of the reality of God and his intimate connection with human affairs. It is
equally apparent that he was more amused than
impressed by the theological distinctions which
characterized his day, and that his one conclusive
test of religious belief was the sort of conduct
that belief produced.

A letter written to his father in 1738 would indicate that his worthy and Puritanic parents were somewhat concerned over the "broadness" of their son who was beginning to be a man of some note in the distant city of Philadelphia.

Philadelphia, April 13, 1738.

Honoured Father,

I have your favours of the 21st of March, in which you both seem concerned lest I have imbibed some erroneous opinions. Doubtless I have my share; and when the natural weakness and imperfection of human understanding is considered, the unavoidable influence of education, custom, books, and company upon our ways of thinking, I imagine a man must have a good deal of vanity who believes, and a good deal of boldness who affirms, that all the doctrines he holds are true, and all he rejects are false. And perhaps the same may be justly said of every sect, church, and society of men, when they assume to themselves that infallibility which they deny to the Pope and councils.

I think opinions should be judged by their influences and effects; and, if a man holds none that tend to make him less virtuous or more vicious, it may be concluded he holds none that are dangerous; which I hope is the case with me.

I am sorry you should have any uneasiness on my account; and if it were a thing possible for one to alter his opinions in order to please another, I know none whom I ought more willingly to oblige in that respect than yourselves. But, since it is no more in a man's power to think than to look like another, methinks all that should be expected from me is to keep my mind open to conviction, to hear patiently and examine attentively, whatever is offered me for that end; and, if after all I continue in the same errors, I believe your usual charity will induce you to rather pity and excuse, than blame me. In the meantime your care and concern for me is what I am very thankful for.

My mother grieves, that one of her sons is an Arian, another an Arminian. What an Arminian or an Arian is, I cannot say that I very well know. The truth is, I make such distinctions very little my study. I think vital religion has always suffered, when orthodoxy is more regarded than virtue; and the Scriptures assure me, that at the last day we shall not be examined for what we thought, but what we did; and our recommendation will not be, that we said, Lord! Lord! but that we did good to our fellow creatures. See Matt. xxv.

I am your dutiful son

B. FRANKLIN.

George Whitefield, the representative in America of the Wesleyan movement in England and an evangelist of persuasive sincerity and amazing eloquence, came to Philadelphia in 1739. The church pulpits were all closed to Whitefield because of the freedom of his speech. As the crowds that wished to hear him were greater than any church would contain, a group of persons voluntarily erected a building one hundred by seventy feet, in which might speak any preacher of any religious persuasion who had something to say to the people of Philadelphia. Knowing Franklin's propensity to follow new and original projects, we are not surprised to find him one of Whitefield's supporters. But he would not back up the great itinerant in his project for an orphanage in Georgia, because of a disagreement in policy.

Whitefield collected considerable money for his enterprises and there were not lacking those who said that much of it found its way into his own pockets. Franklin avows his confidence in Whitefield's integrity and he knew him pretty well on the business side. He says: "He us'd, indeed, sometimes to pray for my conversion, but never had the satisfaction of believing that his prayers were heard. Ours was a mere civil friendship, sincere on both sides, and lasted to his death." One can imagine that this was an odd friendship and yet a real one between two great souls who probably thought nearly alike on essentials and yet were continually disagreeing about details.

"The following instance," says Franklin, "will show something of the terms on which we stood. Upon one of his arrivals from England at Boston, he wrote to me that he should come soon to Philadelphia, but he knew not where he could lodge when there, as he understood his old friend and host, Mr. Benezet, was removed to Germantown. My answer was, 'You know my house; if you can make shift with its scanty accommodations, you will be most heartily welcome.' He replied, that if I made that kind offer for Christ's sake, I should not miss of a reward. And I returned, 'Don't let me be mistaken; it was not for Christ's sake, but for your sake.'" It is abundantly evident that Franklin greatly admired Whitefield because of his sincerity and his ability as a speaker and as a leader.

The letters of this period show that the orthodox members of the Franklin family in Boston were not only genuinely concerned over brother Benjamin's spiritual estate, but sometimes labored with him to the end that he should return to their fold, yet he steadily refused to give over his own views of spiritual things. How could such a refusal be conveyed in a more generous, kindly and really Christian spirit than it was in this reply to his sister Jenny, Mrs. Jane Mecom:

Philadelphia, July 28, 1743.

Dearest Sister Jenny,

I took your admonition very kindly, and was far from being offended at you for it. If I say anything about it to you, it is only to rectify some wrong opinions you seem to have entertained of me; and this I do only because they give you some uneasiness, which I am unwilling to be the occasion of. You express yourself, as if you thought I was against the worshipping of God, and doubt that good works would merit heaven; which are both fancies of your own, I think, without foundation. I am so far from thinking that God is not to be worshipped, that I have composed and wrote a whole book of devotions for my own use; and I imagine there are few if any in the world so weak as to imagine that the little good we can do here can merit so vast a reward hereafter.

There are some things in your New England doctrine and worship, which I do not agree with; but I do not therefore, condemn them, or desire to shake your belief or practice of them. We may dislike things that are nevertheless right in themselves. I would only have you make me the same allowance, and have a better opinion both of morality and your brother. Read the pages of Mr. Edwards's late book, entitled "Some Thoughts concerning the present Revival of Religion in New England," from 367 to 375, and when you judge of others if you can perceive the fruit to be good, don't terrify yourself that the tree may be evil; but be assured it is not so, for you know who has said, "Men do not gather grapes of thorns and figs of thistles." I have no time to add, but that I shall always be your affectionate brother,

B. FRANKLIN.

We shall see in later pages that one of Franklin's distinguishing traits was his toleration of the opinions of others. He did not permit the fact that his "Dearest Sister Jenny" took him to task most vigorously for his deviation from her standards of orthodoxy, to make any sort of breach between them. He had the art of differing with others and at the same time maintaining intact the bonds of affection. The latter he, no doubt, considered the more important. At any rate, he kept up a continued correspondence with his sister and did not shy at the subject of religion. One cannot help but fancy that Jenny came to think more generously of her broad-minded brother, and to value greatly such a letter as the following, which he wrote her from London some fifteen years later.

London, September 16, 1758.

Dear Sister,

I received your favor of June 17. I wonder you have had no letter from me since my being in England.

I congratulate you on the conquest of Cape Breton, and hope as your people took it by praying, the first time, you will now pray that it may never be given up again, which you then forgot.

Our cousin Jane Franklin, daughter of our uncle John, died about a year ago. We saw her husband, Robert Page, who gave us some old letters to his wife, from Uncle Benjamin. In one

of them, dated Boston, July 4, 1723, he writes
that your uncle Josiah has a daughter Jane, about
twelve years old, a good humoured child. So
keep up to your character, and don't be angry
when you have no letters. In a little book he
sent her, called "None but Christ," he wrote an
acrostick on her name, which for namesake's
sake, as well as the good advice it contains, I
transcribe and send you, viz.:

> Illumined from on high,
> And shining brightly in your sphere,
> Ne'er faint, but keep a steady eye,
> Expecting endless pleasures there.
>
> Flee vice as you'd a serpent flee;
> Raise faith, and hope three stories higher,
> And let Christ's endless love to thee
> Ne'er cease to make thy love aspire.
> Kindness of heart by words express,
> Let your obedience be sincere,
> In prayer and praise your God address
> Nor cease, till he can cease to hear.

After professing truly that I had a great es-
teem and veneration for the pious author, permit
me a little to play the commentator and critic on
these lines. The meaning of three stories higher

seems somewhat obscure. You are to understand, then, that faith, hope, and charity have been called the three steps of Jacob's ladder, reaching from earth to heaven; our author calls them stories, likening religion to a building, and these are the three stories of the Christian edifice. Faith is then the ground floor, hope is up one pair of stairs. My dear beloved Jenny, don't delight so much to dwell in those lower rooms, but get as fast as you can into the garret, for in truth the best room in the house is charity. For my part, I wish the house was turned upside down; 'tis so difficult (when one is fat) to go upstairs; and not only so, but I imagine hope and faith may be more firmly built upon charity, than charity upon faith and hope. However that may be, I think it the better reading to say

Raise faith and hope one story higher,

Correct it boldly, and I'll support the alteration; for, when you are up two stories already, if you raise your building three stories higher you will make five in all, which is two more than there should be, you expose your upper rooms more to the winds and storms; and, besides I am afraid the foundation will hardly bear them, unless indeed you build with such light stuff as straw and

stubble, and that, you know, won't stand fire.
Again, where the author says,

> Kindness of heart by words express,

strike out words, and put deeds. The world is
too full of compliments already. They are the
rank growth of every soil, and choak the good
plants of benevolence, and beneficence; nor do I
pretend to be the first in this comparison of words
and actions to plants; you may remember an an-
cient poet, whose works we have all studied and
copied at school long ago:

> A man of words and not of deeds
> Is like a garden full of weeds.

'Tis a pity that good works, among some sorts
of people, are so little valued, and good words
admired in their stead; I mean seemingly pious
discourses, instead of humaine benevolent actions.
Those they almost put out of countenance, by call-
ing morality rotten morality, righteousness rag-
ged righteousness, and even filthy rags—and
when you mention virtue, pucker up their noses
as if they smelt a stink; at the same time that
they eagerly snuff up an empty canting harangue,
as if it was a posey of the choicest flowers.

B. FRANKLIN.

There is all through this letter that characteristic, and delightful mingling of raillery and
serious meaning that make Franklin's letters such
incomparable reading. The theological distinctions between imputed righteousness and good
works that were prevalent in his day and for
many a day afterward were to him all of a piece
with that "great uncertainty" that he had found
in metaphysical reasonings long years before,
and because of which he had quitted them for
others more satisfactory.

The strictly orthodox mind cannot easily grasp
the vision of those bolder souls, who have a tre-
mendous consciousness of the part that a living
God plays in human affairs, and who pray to that
God with all fervor, and at the same time con-
centrate all possible energy, precaution, and effort to accomplish the aim of that prayer. The
apparent contradiction of faith and works that
called forth the ironic comment of St. James,
*"Show me thy faith apart from thy works, and I
by my works will show thee my faith,"* was the
occasion of a similar reply from Benjamin to his
brother John (who was evidently engaged in
solving one of the knotty problems of the Third
Intercolonial War). You can almost see the

amiable little wrinkles in the corner of the philosopher's eye as he pens this to Brother John:

Philadelphia, [Mar. 10] 1745.

Our people are extremely impatient to hear of your success at Cape Breton. My shop is filled with thirty inquirers at the coming in of every post. Some wonder the place is not yet taken. I tell them I shall be glad to hear that news three months hence. Fortified towns are hard nuts to crack; and your teeth have not been accustomed to it. Taking strong places is a particular trade, which you have taken up without serving an apprenticeship to it. Armies and veterans need skilful engineers to direct them in their attack. Have you any? But some seem to think forts are as easy taken as snuff. Father Moody's prayers look tolerably modest. You have a fast and prayer day for that purpose; in which I compute five hundred thousand petitions were offered up to the same effect in New England, which added to the petitions of every family morning and evening, multiplied by the number of days since January 25th, make forty-five millions of prayers; which, set against the prayers of a few priests in the garrison, to the Virgin Mary, give a vast balance in your favor.

If you do not succeed, I fear I shall have but an indifferent opinion of Presbyterian prayers in such cases, as long as I live. Indeed, in attacking strong towns I should have more dependence on works, than on faith; for, like the kingdom of heaven, they are to be taken by force and violence; and in a French garrison I suppose there are devils of that kind, that they are not to be cast out by prayers and fasting, unless it be by their own fasting for want of provisions. I believe there is Scripture in what I have wrote, but I cannot adorn that margin with quotations, having a bad memory, and no Concordance at hand; besides no more time than to subscribe myself, etc.

B. Franklin.

Probably brother John thought that Benjamin was close to blasphemy when he read this letter that ridiculed him for expecting to take a walled and defended city by prayers rather than engineering skill. Yet Benjamin believed in praying though his general philosophy of it was far less mechanical and much truer according to modern thinking than the orthodox opinion of his day would allow.

What a thinking man's real religious feeling

may be seldom appears, certainly not advantageously, in letters of even a semicontroversial sort like these to his critical family. The atmosphere of unfavorable criticism does not permit the blossoming of those gentler and truer flowers of the heart that show their real beauty, and give their richest fragrance only in a kindlier air. There is one letter of Franklin's that opens the inner door of his heart, and discloses its true inspiring motive. There is in it no dogma; one may be permitted to doubt if there is ever any taint of dogma in the real spirit of the Christ. One can only say that if any fair proportion of men could write a letter similar to this, the darkness of our whole confused world would be well on the way to disappearance in a dawning of a brighter civilization. For let us not forget that the basis of real civilization is being civil, one man to another. The letter was written to Joseph Huey, when Franklin was about forty-seven years old.

Philadelphia, June 6, 1753.

Sir,

As to the kindness you mention, I wish it could have been of more service to you. But if it had, the only thanks I should desire is, that you would always be equally ready to serve any other person that may need your assistance, and so let good offices go round, for mankind are all of a family.

For my own part, when I am employed in serving others, I do not look upon myself as conferring favors, but as paying debts. In my travels, and since my settlement, I have received much kindness from men, to whom I shall never have any opportunity of making the least direct return. And numberless mercies from God, who is infinitely above being benefited by our services. Those kindnesses from man, I can therefore only return on their fellow men; and I can only show my gratitude for these mercies from God, by a readiness to help his other children and my brethren. For I do not think that thanks and compliments, tho' repeated weekly, can discharge our real obligations to each other, and much less those to our Creator. You will see in this my notion of good works, that I am far from expecting (as you suppose) to merit Heaven by them. By Heaven we understand a state of happiness, infinite in degree, and eternal in duration: I can do nothing to deserve such rewards. He that for giving a draught of water to a thirsty person, should expect to be paid with a good plantation, would be modest in his demands,

compar'd with those who think they deserve
Heaven for the little good they do on earth.
Even the mix'd imperfect pleasures we enjoy in
this world, are rather from God's goodness than
our merit; how much more such happiness of
Heaven. For my own part I have not the vanity
to think I deserve it, the folly to expect it, nor
the ambition to desire it; but content myself in
submitting to the will and disposal of that God
who made me, who has hitherto preserv'd and
bless'd me, and in whose Fatherly goodness I
may well confide, that he will never make me
miserable, and that even the afflictions I may at
any time suffer shall tend to my benefit.

The faith you mention has doubtless its use in
the world. I do not desire to see it diminished,
nor would I endeavor to lessen it in any man.
But I wish it were more productive of good
works than I have generally seen it: I mean
real good works, works of kindness, charity,
mercy, and public spirit; not holiday-keeping,
sermon-reading or hearing, performing church
ceremonies, or making long prayers, filled with
flatteries and compliments, despis'd even by wise
men, and much less capable of pleasing the Deity.
The worship of God is a duty; the hearing and
reading of sermons may be useful; but, if men

rest in hearing and praying, as too many do, it is as if a tree should value itself on being water'd and putting forth leaves, tho' it never produc'd any fruit.

Your great Master tho't much less of these outward appearances and professions than many of his modern disciples. He prefer'd the *doers* of the Word, to the mere *hearers;* the son that seemingly refus'd to obey his father, and yet perform'd his commands, to him that profess'd his readiness, but neglected the work; the heretical but charitable Samaritan, to the uncharitable tho' orthodox priest and sanctified Levite; and those who gave food to the hungry, drink to the thirsty, raiment to the naked, entertainment to the stranger; and relief to the sick, tho' they never heard of his name, he declared shall in the last day be accepted, when those who cry Lord! Lord! who value themselves on their faith, tho' great enough to perform miracles, but have neglected good works, shall be rejected. He profess'd, that he came not to call the righteous but Sinners to repentance; which imply'd his modest opinion, that there were some in his time so good, that they need not hear even him for improvement; but now-a-days we have scarce a little parson, that does not think it the duty of every man within his reach to sit under his petty ministrations; and that whoever omits them offends God. I wish to such more humility, and to you health and happiness, being your friend and servant,

B. FRANKLIN.

There is in this letter none of the ridicule that besprinkles some of those written to members of his family but there is the same condemnation of the orthodox religious thinking of his day, and the same suppressed resentment at the futility of so many of the ministers. There is really nothing very obscure about Franklin's religious beliefs at this period of his life. He had no theology but he had a great deal of the humanitarian spirit of the New Testament.

The casual reader of the *Autobiography* can gain at best only a partial view of the real character of the author. It does not, as indeed such a record cannot, convey the accurate picture of the writer's character that an honest and painstaking biographer might. However, one suspects that truthful biographies are the work of the recording angel alone. All human biographers begin with some bias for or against their subject; if they are entirely neutral their work is dull. Something of the same inadequacy holds true of an autobiographer as well, and while Franklin's is one of the best, we would not know him as he really was if the *Autobiography* were all that we possessed. His letters (and where was there ever his superior as a letter writer?), like the successive touches of the artist's brush, fill in the real picture of which the *Autobiography* is only a rude sketch. We must remember that the *Autobiography* was begun when he was sixty-five; that it was written at odd times, and was not finished till he was eighty-two, and even then brought the record down only to 1757, when the really significant part of his life as a public servant and diplomat had not yet begun.

Not a little of the anxiety of the family in Boston was caused, no doubt, by the fact that Benjamin had deserted the Presbyterian church in favor of the Episcopal. The *Autobiography* gives no hint of this, and leaves one with the impression that in middle life he quite gave over churchgoing. There is good evidence that he held a pew in Christ Church, Philadelphia, from 1760 to the time of his death in 1790. A special committee was appointed by the Rector, Dr. Dorr, in 1863, to inquire into the location of the pew which, according to tradition, was occupied by both Washington and Franklin. This committee reported that the pew occupied by Franklin was evidently the one then numbered 25 in the center aisle. On the ground plan of the church made in 1760 it was numbered 59. Franklin's name appears in the pewbooks as a renter of three seats in this pew until the time of his death in 1790. In all probability he was an occupant for many years previous to 1760, but as the pewbooks of earlier date were not to be found, the committee could give no data relative to it. Franklin's name, however, appears in the minutes of the vestry as early as 1739, when he subscribed to the fund raised for the completion of the new church building. Again in 1751 he subscribed for the erection of the steeple and the purchase of bells. In 1752 the vestry appointed him one of thirteen managers of a lottery for the raising of money to finish the steeple and the purchase of a chime of bells. He was reappointed the following year. The inference was, therefore, that Franklin occupied the pew in question during these successive years. After his death the pew was transferred to his son-in-law, Richard Bache.

Whether Franklin habitually or only occasionally occupied this pew is, of course, a question, though certainly his occupancy could not have been for very long. From 1757 to 1762 he was in England and again from 1764 to 1775, and from December 1776 to 1785 he was in France. I hazard the easy guess that during this long tenancy of the pew in Christ Church it was oftener used by the family than by its distinguished head. The above mentioned report does show, however, that he maintained to his death a regard for public worship. If we should need further evidence of the value he placed on churchgoing we should have it in a letter to his daughter, Sarah, written in 1764. This may properly be taken as indicating Franklin's opinion on the value of churchgoing when he was a man of fifty-eight.

My dear child, the natural prudence and goodness of heart God has blest you with make it less necessary for me to be particular in giving you advice. I shall therefore only say, that the more attentively dutiful and tender you are towards your good mamma, the more you will recommend yourself to me. But why should I mention *me,* when you have so much higher a promise in the commandments, that such conduct will recommend you to the favor of God? You know I have many enemies, all indeed on the public account, (for I cannot recollect that I have in a private capacity given just cause of offence to any one whatever), yet they are enemies, and very bitter ones; and you must expect their enmity will extend in some degree to you, so that your slightest indiscretions will be magnified into crimes, in order the more sensibly to wound and afflict me. It is therefore the more necessary for you to be extremely circumspect in all your behaviour, that no advantage may be given to their malevolence.

Go constantly to church, whoever preaches. The act of devotion in the common prayer book is your principal business there, and if properly attended to, will do more towards amending the heart than sermons generally can do. For they were composed by men of much greater piety and wisdom than our common composers of sermons can pretend to be; and therefore I wish you would never miss the prayer days; yet I do not mean you should despise sermons, even of the preachers you dislike, for the discourse is often much better than the man, as sweet and clear waters come through very dirty earth. I am the more particular on this head, as you seemed to express a little before I came away some inclination to leave our church, which I would not have you do.

His advice to Sarah was not of the sort that is sometimes given to others and not followed by the giver himself. Franklin always liked a good sermon. He not only had many close personal friends among preachers of various affiliations, but he went to hear them preach. Such a letter as the following to Dr. Richard Price indicates that he had a strong preference for the type of sermon that he should hear from him. Price was a man of a high order of intellect and was widely known in his generation for his writings on political and financial questions. His pamphlet on "Observations on Civil Liberty and the Justice and Policy of the War with America," is said to have had a considerable share in determining the Americans to declare their independence. It would be interesting if we could know what Sunday trips Franklin and Sir John Pringle took to various churches about London to hear preachers who represented "rational Christianity." That such trips were made we cannot doubt.

To RICHARD PRICE
Craven Street, Sept. 18, 1772.

Dear Sir,

Inclos'd I send you Dr. Priestly's last letter. If he had come to town, and preach'd here sometimes, I fancy Sir John P. would now and then have been one of his hearers; for he likes his theology as well as his philosophy. Sir John has asked me if I knew where he could go to hear a preacher of *rational* Christianity. I told him I knew several of them, but did not know where their churches were in town; out of town, I mentioned yours at Newington, and offered to go with him. He agreed to it, but said we should first let you know our intention. I suppose, if nothing in his profession prevents, we may come, if you please, next Sunday; but if you sometimes preach in town, that will be most convenient to him, and I request you would by a line let me know when and where. If there are dissenting preachers of that sort at this end of the town, I wish you would recommend one to me, naming the place of his meeting. And if you please, give me a list of several in different parts of the town, perhaps he may incline to take a round among them. At present I believe he has no view of attending constantly anywhere, but now and then only as it may suit his convenience. . . .

Yours most affectionately,

B. FRANKLIN.

Franklin's attitude toward churches has been baffling to many because while he evidently is not an ardent adherent of any church, and finds something to criticize in many of them, he is nevertheless a pew holder in a church most of his life and his name appears as a donor to many churches of many different forms of belief.

Nothing could be more wide of the mark than to place him with those who sit in "the seat of the scornful," or to conceive him as courting popularity by his widespread gifts, after the manner of the politician. He had the profoundest respect for religion as religion, but he had a half-amused, half-irritated feeling over the nonessentials that divided men into sects. He was no sectarian. Franklin was scarcely even a thoroughgoing nationalist. He could never be found in the shouting, flag-waving crowd. The great virtues and values that he found in England and France he did not deny or belittle, nor did he ever think to exalt the colonies by deriding the older countries. His attitude was singularly universal. To him a man was a man; a nation was a nation, and a sect was a sect—each a part of a whole and to be valued as such. This explains why he aided so many religious organizations although he never gave any indication that he was in agreement with them.

An interesting instance of his feeling about creeds and their influence appears in an encounter with the leader of a group of Dunkers. It seems that the Dunkers had been the object of certain scandalous misrepresentations, and Franklin advised their leader to publish a creed that would set the public right as to their belief and observances. The Dunkers objected, saying that they hoped for still further disclosures of truth, and that if they were to print their confession of faith they might feel themselves bound, and confined by it. This attitude greatly impressed Franklin; so much so that he wrote, "This modesty in a sect is perhaps the singular instance in the history of mankind; every other sect supposing itself in possession of all truth, and that those who differ are so far in the wrong; like a man travelling in foggy weather; those at some distance before him on the road he sees wrapped in the fog, as well as those behind him, and also people in the fields on each side; but near him all appear clear; though in truth he is as much in the fog as any of them."

Even more than in his gifts, Franklin's fundamental sympathy with religion is evidenced by his willingness to print the sermons and tracts of the various bodies that sought him as a publisher. It would be going pretty far to say that he did this wholly from benevolence. Though he was paid for them, nevertheless the profits on such publications were necessarily small and the circulation sure to be limited. Such publications would be quite unattractive to the publisher who was not in sympathy with his clients.

The list of the religious publications bearing Franklin's imprint is interesting, and almost imposing. Surely if he read a fraction of them he was well saturated with sound doctrine of all sorts. Here we find "A Sermon on the Important Doctrine of Regeneration," by William Dewsbury. The title page states that it was taken from his mouth in shorthand. William Dewsbury was a Quaker.

Another sermon is entitled "Christ Triumphing and Satan Raging," by Samuel Finlay. What Finlay's religious connection may have been does not appear. A glimpse of the writing would lead one to think that he was an outsider and remonstrant-in-general. We are not surprised at finding a long list of sermons, letters, and volumes of sermons by his friend the Reverend George Whitefield.

"A Confession of Faith," drawn up apparently by some English Baptists and adopted by the Philadelphia Baptist Association in 1742, was printed by Franklin in 1743. It would be a surprise to many a good Baptist to learn that the celebrated Philadelphia Confession was first printed in America by Franklin.

Equally surprising it might be to many a good Presbyterian to learn that Jonathan Edwards' sermons, when published, frequently bore the imprint of Franklin. Two minds could scarcely be at greater divergence than those of Jonathan Edwards and Benjamin Franklin, yet they started from the same base, a very real and profound belief in the reality of God. Each mind greatly influenced our national life and as between the two the average modern Christian is probably nearer Franklin's conception of God than Edwards'.

It was an age of strong convictions, and we find that Franklin's press was responsible for not a few publications like "Clear Light Put Out in Obscure Darkness," by Samuel Finlay; "Remarks upon Mr. Whitefield," (proving him a man under delusion) by G. Gillespie; "A Call to the Unfaithful Professors of Truth," and an overwhelming number of blasts and counterblasts be-

A
CONFESSION
OF
FAITH,

Put forth by the
Elders and *Brethren*
Of many
CONGREGATIONS
OF
CHRISTIANS

(Baptized upon Profession of their Faith)
In *London* and the *Country*.

Adopted by the Baptist ASSOCIATION
met at Philadelphia, Sept. 25. 1742.

The SIXTH EDITION.

To which are added,
Two Articles *viz.* Of Imposition of Hands,
and Singing of Psalms in Publick Worship.
ALSO
A Short Treatise of Church Discipline.

With the Heart Man believeth unto Righteousness, and with the Mouth Confession is made unto Salvation, Rom. 10. 20.
Search the Scriptures, John 5. 39.

PHILADELPHIA: Printed by B. FRANKLIN.
M,DCC,XLIII.

tween the defenders of Free Grace on one side, and Predestination on the other.

Most of these, happily, died at one printing. Much more long-lived have been the longer and shorter catechisms of the Presbyterian Church and "A New Version of the Psalms of David" fitted to the times, used in churches, by N. Brady, D.D., and N. Tate, Esq. There was also a considerable list of devotional books like "The Directory for Family Worship, Approved by the General Assembly of the Church of Scotland" and "Devout Exercises of the Heart," by E. Rowe.

The total list of Franklin imprints discloses the fact that more than 75 per cent were of a religious character though of course the bulk of his work, counting by pages, was of a public nature. Manifestly, our subject had a large share in the spreading of religion in his day by the printed page.

One of Franklin's most charming traits was his genius for making and preserving friendships. Where to-day do we find a man on whose shoulders rest the most vital of international relations, who yet has time for scientific investigations and for long chatty letters, serious, gay, argumentative, friendly—and *all written with his own hand?*

It is a tempting theme, we leave it with regret, but one must resist its allurement, and return to the proposed task of uncovering, if possible, the view of his religion. Among his correspondents are many men who held priestly office. In England from 1764 to 1775, when he was fighting the losing battle for a reconciliation between Parliament and the Colonies, Dr. Priestly was one of his warm friends and good counselors. An irreligious or irreverent man, or even one who was unsympathetic with religious things, would never have had such a delightful intimacy with Dr. Shipley, the good Bishop of Asaph, as Franklin had. The Bishop and his family on their part seem to have had a high appreciation of Franklin's company and correspondence. He was often a guest at their home and his letters written to various members of the family are some of the most delightful we have. Among them is one on "The Art of Procuring Pleasant Dreams." The exigencies of the Great War brought out for sale for the benefit of the Red Cross a beautifully bound portfolio from the library of the Shipley family in which are a dozen autograph letters of Franklin's including "The Art of Procuring Pleasant Dreams," written in his most charming vein to Catherine Shipley. It is not amiss in our present inquiry to observe also that the conclusion of that celebrated skit reads:

These are the rules of the art. But, though they will generally prove effectual in producing the end intended, there is a case in which the most punctual observance of them will be totally fruitless. I need not mention the case to you, my dear friend, but my account of the art would be imperfect without it. The case is, when the person who desires to have pleasant dreams has not taken care to preserve, what is necessary above all things, A GOOD CONSCIENCE.

There is a rare beauty in the correspondence which was maintained betwen Franklin and the Shipleys throughout the entire period of the war separating their two countries. After the father's death Franklin continued the correspondence with the daughter, Catherine Shipley, even after his own return to Philadelphia. In a letter written from Passy, June 10, 1782, to Bishop Shipley, Franklin said: "There never has been or ever will be any such thing *as a good war or a bad peace.*" This is not the only occasion when he made use of this phrase. We cannot be sure that it is original with him, though it may have been, but in many of his letters written during the war with England he makes use of the same words. Where could he have forged a better weapon to fight the belligerent ideas and wasteful errors of his contemporaries? Among the most definite teachings of Jesus was, "Blessed are the peacemakers," and no statesman ever lived who more clearly saw the folly of warfare than did Franklin, or sacrificed himself more completely in the effort to avert war and make peace. We may unhesitatingly credit to him in full measure the virtue of the peacemaker.

The cycle of history constantly turns up problems and proposals that appear to be entirely new and distinctly modern yet which on closer study are found to be rooted in the forgotten past. The press of all sorts, since the close of the World War, has been filled with discussions of a League of Nations, the most acute angle of which has been the relations between England, France, and America. How astonished some of the opponents of such a combination would be to learn that Franklin entertained the thought of such a three-cornered alliance in 1783, as indicated in a letter written by him to David Hartley.

Passy, Oct. 16, 1783.

My dear Friend,

I think with you, that your Quaker article is a good one, and that men will in time have sense enough to adopt it, but I fear that time is not yet come.

What would you think of a proposition, if I sh'd make it, of a family compact between England, France and America? America w'd be as happy as the Sabine Girls, if she c'd be the means of uniting in perpetual peace her father and her husband. What repeated follies are these repeated wars! You do not want to conquer & govern one another. Why then sh'd you continually be employed in injuring & destroying one another? How many excellent things might have been done to promote the internal welfare of each country; what bridges, roads, canals, and other useful public works & institutions, tending to the common felicity, might have been made and established with the money and men foolishly spent during the last seven centuries by our mad wars in doing one another mischief! You are near neighbors, and each have very respectable qualities. Learn to be quiet and to respect each other's rights.   You are all Christians.   One is *The Most Christian King,* and the other *Defender of the Faith.*   Manifest the propriety of these titles by your future conduct.   "By this," says Christ, "shall all men know that ye are my Disciples if ye love one another."   "Seek peace, and ensue it."   Adieu.

Yours most affectionately,

B. FRANKLIN.

There were very few men in public life in 1783 who were in the least disposed to condemn war as war.   Apparently the conception that there was anything at all inconsistent between war and Christianity had not arrived in the public mind. But it had arrived in Franklin's mind.   He would be called a pacifist in some quarters to-day.   He saw clearly that Christ's principles and war were absolute opposites.   This is another evidence of the projecting quality of his religious thinking. He was as advanced here as in his scientific thinking and in his public enterprises.

Among the prominent men in American church history who were his close friends and correspondents, mention may be made of Dr. Benjamin Rush, of Philadelphia, and Dr. Ezra Stiles, president of Yale College, who was recommended by

Franklin for the degree of Doctor of Laws which he received from the University of St. Andrews in 1759. In a letter to Dr. Stiles, written in the closing year of his life, Franklin says of himself: "All sects here, and we have a great variety, have experienced my good will in assisting them with subscriptions for building their new places of worship; and, as I have never opposed any of their doctrines, I hope to go out of the world in peace with them all."

Here again we get the note of the antisectarian, though now in old age the sharpness has gone. It is characteristic of Franklin, however, that even in old age he has not altered his opinion. Once having come to a conclusion Franklin seldom altered it for the rest of his life.

The world would be infinitely the richer if the men it calls great might with freedom write their own life story as did Benjamin Franklin. Yet the world is poor in good autobiography, which is partially a tribute to the natural modesty of great souls, and partly, no doubt, due to the fear that if they tell the real truth about their lives, they will be seriously misjudged and misrepresented. Yet if they tell not the flat truth, there is little enthusiasm for the telling at all.

One cannot help but feel that Franklin's reputation has suffered greatly by the natural propensity of human nature to magnify faults and minimize virtues when a man confesses to both. Franklin has told the bald truth about the errata of his early life, and, in the minds of many, these errata have been enlarged to cover a lifetime which they mention with a sigh and a smile as if his life were a long series of escapades and infidelities.

The facts of the case do not bear this out. Franklin confessed his youthful errata and made reparation of them in just so far as he was able. His letters and autobiography abound in direct statements of so high a moral and religious standard that he would without doubt be reported as in good and regular standing in most churches of to-day. How it is possible for a historian to say, as some have said, that Franklin was irreligious, it is difficult to understand. He was not religious if we measure him by the standards of men like George Whitefield or Dr. Stiles, but if we compare him with the public men of his time we will find that he gave much more thought than the average layman of his day to religious things. We might almost assert that few public men in modern history have given evidence of as much clear thought about spiritual things, and almost none have been equally willing to record their convictions so frankly.

Very early in his young manhood he made a creed for himself. It would seem as if, when he felt that he could no longer accept the creed of his fathers and knew no other church to whose creed he could subscribe, he was unwilling to be branded as a total unbeliever because that was not the truth, and so he made his own creed. This, too, is characteristic of him. Although he was preëminently social and friendly, Franklin was apparently perfectly willing to be alone in his opinions and convictions. He could hold them in this solitary fashion without becoming either a propagandist or a combatant.

The creed is another example of the continuity of Franklin's convictions, because while he drew it up in his youth he declared his allegiance to it at various times throughout his life, notably in a letter to Madam Brillon, written from Passy in 1781, at which time he was seventy-five years old. The creed was as follows:

That there is one God who made all Things
That he governs the world by his providence
That he ought to be worshiped by adoration
    Prayer and Thanksgiving

But that the most acceptable service to God is
     doing good to men
That the soul is immortal
And that God will certainly reward virtue and
     punish vice
Either here or hereafter.

This statement sounds fairly generous to modern ears but there was not, in Franklin's day, any
church that could have admitted him to member-
ship in good standing on such a confession. It is
mostly an Old Testament creed for it is lacking in
those distinctive things that are taught in the
New Testament, except his faith in the immortality of he soul, which teaching is largely absent from the Old Testament. The truly Christian Creed centers mostly about the person of
Jesus Christ and his offices in bringing together
men and their creator. The redemptive work of
Christ found no place in Franklin's belief though
he did have opinions about Christ. He knew the
New Testament as well as the Old.

Every man does his thinking in the terms of
his own age—is, in fact, a "prisoner of his age"—
and Franklin was no exception to this rule. All
his letters, his prayer book, and this creed show
very markedly the influence of the Deistic think-

ing current in his day. In any attempt to analyze his religion we must take into account those books against Deism that he read in his youth. We unfortunately do not know what the books were, but we do know the main currents of the Deism that was current in his time.

The Deism of Franklin's generation was revolt against tradition, supernaturalism, and literalism. Consider for a moment what orthodoxy meant. Here is a clause from the Athanasian Creed:

Whosoever will be saved, before all things it is necessary that he hold the catholic faith; which faith, except every one to keep whole and undefiled, without doubt he shall perish everlastingly. And the catholic faith is this: that we worship one God in trinity and trinity in unity; neither confounding the persons nor dividing the substance. For there is one person of the Father, another of the Son and another of the Holy Ghost. But the Godhead of the Father, of the Son, and of the Holy Ghost is all one; the glory equal, the majesty co-eternal. Such as the Father is, such is the Son and such is the Holy Ghost— uncreate, incomprehensible, eternal. The Father is made of none, neither created nor begotten. The Son is of the Father alone, neither made nor created, but begotten. The Holy Ghost is of the Father and the Son; neither made nor created nor begotten but proceeding.

The imagination staggers at the attempt to conceive of Franklin's trying to say "Credo" to that.

The Deists simply revolted at anything of the kind and proceeded to express religion in terms of the new and reasonable universe in which they found themselves. Rapid advance had been made in scientific knowledge. The world was no longer flat but placed securely in a revolving universe. The fascinating discoveries of Newton and others in the sphere of natural science had swept miracles entirely away. The Bible was no longer conceived of as a magic book. Orthodoxy taught a conception of inspiration that made every Biblical writer little more than an acquiescent amanuensis, and the results of his writing were providentially preserved free from error. This conception of the Bible also had to give way before the new revelations of science for many of these views were simply untenable in the light of the new knowledge.

Along with this, the confidence in institutions waned and the tide rose in favor of individualism.

A CALL

TO THE

Unfaithful Proffesors

OF

TRUTH.

WRITTEN BY

JOHN ESTAUGH

In his Life-time; and now Publifhed
for General Service.

TO WHICH IS ADDED

Divers EPISTLES

Of the fame AUTHOR.

PHILADELPHIA:
Printed by B. FRANKLIN,
M,DCC,XLIV.

There was a pronounced tendency to accept reason, and reason alone, as authoritative.

The Deists were not Atheists; differing as they did about many things, they were in entire agreement in affirming the reality of a Creator of our Universe, supreme in power and perfect in goodness. But intoxicated with the splendor of the new-found "natural law" they denied that he had any providential relations with the world. Some of them called themselves Christians, because they believed Jesus to be the great teacher of spiritual and moral truth, but they did not for a moment accept the creeds that purported to describe his relations to the Godhead.

The Deists were not irreligious; while they felt that particular forms of worship were nonessential, yet worship itself was not only a duty but a necessity, it must take the form of piety and virtue. True religion meant to project one's life on the lines of reason which to them meant the very thought and will of God. Practically all Deists taught faith in the immortality of the soul and the certainty of future rewards and punishments.

Much of this sounds very familiar to our ears, for the Deist headed the revolt within the Christian body that has greatly affected the history of Christian thinking in our own day.

To understand Franklin, therefore, we must conceive of his mind as being steeped during all its earlier years in the most rigid school of orthodoxy and virtue and then suddenly plunged into the rationalistic atmosphere of the Deistic thinking of his day. He came out neither a Deist nor an orthodox churchman.

We have a habit of looking for labels for men. Labels are convenient. They save thinking, an economy that most of us are ever ready to practice. But we cannot put a label on Franklin. It would not stick. He was not a Deist, the influence of his childhood preserved for him a vivid belief in the providential care of God. He was not a churchman, because the organized church was to him sacred only because of its reasonableness. The cross of Christ, so far as we know, meant nothing to him except a demonstration of God's affectionate regard. Anything like the normal Christian experience of repentance, confession, and a sense of forgiveness we look for in vain in his writings. Yet with all these deficiencies from the normal experience, Franklin did surely exhibit a rich number of the virtues that Christianity has always called her choicest fruits. And as he said so often, "Do men gather grapes of thorns or figs of thistles?"

The creed that he adhered to all his life shows the traces of his spiritual background and development.

For various reasons Franklin refused to be drawn into religious controversy, but on safe occasions he did not hesitate to speak his mind with admirable candor.

When he was eighty-four years old, Dr. Stiles, President of Yale College, wrote him requesting a portrait for the walls of the college, and in his letter said that he had never known his religious beliefs and asked Franklin to express them. "I wish," he said, "to know the opinion of my venerable friend, concerning Jesus of Nazareth. He will not impute this to impertinence or improper curiosity in one, who for so many years has continued to love, estimate, and reverence his abilities and literary character, with an ardor and affection bordering on adoration." Franklin replied by saying that this was the first time that he had ever been questioned on this subject and gave in answer the creed that we have already before us, adding, "As to Jesus of Nazareth, my opinion of whom you particularly desire, I think the system of morals and his religion, as he left them to us, the best the world ever saw or is likely to see; but I apprehend it has received various corrupting changes, and I have, with most of the present dissenters in England, some doubts as to his divinity; tho' it is a question I do not dogmatize upon, having never studied it, and think it needless to busy myself with it now, when I expect soon an opportunity of knowing the truth with less trouble. I see no harm, however, in its being believed, if that belief has the good consequence, as probably it has, of making his doctrines more respected and better observed; especially as I do not perceive, that the Supreme takes it amiss, by distinguishing the unbelievers in his government of the world with any peculiar marks of his displeasure.

"I shall only add, respecting myself, that, having experienced the goodness of that Being in conducting me prosperously thro' a long life, I have no doubt of its continuance in the next, though without the smallest conceit of meriting such goodness."

This latter paragraph we find in substance in more than one of Franklin's letters. One is inclined to take with a little latitude his statement that this was the first time he had ever been asked for his position in regard to orthodox Christianity.

Equally interesting with his creed was Franklin's ingenious scheme for arriving at moral perfection. When he was about twenty-six years old he says that he conceived such a "bold and arduous project." It would have daunted many a bolder soul than his, and eventually he found, he says, that he had "undertaken a task of more difficulty than I imagined." The interesting fact is that Franklin should have conceived of such a program and that he was in such real earnest about moral improvement that he deliberately put his scheme to the test of actual practice. He was always more of a scientist than a theologian and this project makes a good deal more of the scientific experiment on a character than a devout longing after holiness. Either he had a good character in the first place or these moral gymnastics had definite results, because in after life he showed evidence of having acquired to a high degree many of these thirteen selected virtues. The thirteen that he selected were:

1. Temperance—Eat not to dullness; drink not to elevation.

2. Silence—Speak not but what may benefit others or yourself; avoid trifling conversation.

3. Order—Let all your things have their places; let each part of your business have its time.

4. Resolution—Resolve to perform what you ought; perform without fail what you resolve.

5. Frugality—Make no expense but to do good to others or yourself; *i. e.* waste nothing.

6. Industry—Lose no time; be always employed in something useful; cut off all unnecessary actions.

7. Sincerity—Use no hurtful deceits; think innocently and justly, and, if you speak, speak accordingly.

8. Justice—Wrong none by doing injuries or omitting the benefits that are your duty.

9. Moderation—Avoid extremes; forbear resenting injuries so much as you think they deserve.

10. Cleanliness—Tolerate no uncleanliness in body, cloaths or habitation.

11. Tranquillity—Be not disturbed at trifles, or at accidents common or unavoidable.

12. Chastity—Rarely use venery but for health or offspring, never to dullness, weakness, or the injury of your own or another's peace or reputation.

13. Humility—Imitate Jesus and Socrates.

That he did make a determined effort to carry his ambitious ideal into execution he assures us in a further word about it. He made a little book in which he allotted a page for each of the virtues separately, ruling each page with red ink so as to have seven columns, one for each day of the week. He then gave a week's strict attention to each virtue as a beginning. The result of his attempt he records thus: "I enter'd upon the execution of this plan for self-examination, and continu'd it with occasional intermissions for some time. I was surpris'd to find myself so much fuller of faults than I had imagined; but I had the satisfaction of seeing them diminish."

The writer has no desire to make out a "case" for Franklin, but the query has often arisen in his mind why it is that so many writers have noted this attempt at the thirteen virtues with something approaching amusement but very few of them note his creed or his church attendance or the many other records that he has left us of his spiritual convictions such as we have in the letter to David Huey.

It is almost a superfluity to say that Franklin was no Puritan, yet he had the strictest sort of Puritan ancestry and upbringing in his boyhood, the effect of which never left him. Indeed it could not have left him, unless Solomon and all the school of modern psychologists are hopelessly wrong about the effect of bringing up a child in the way he should go.

The Puritan background of fixed determination to do what is right and true, like red under gold, shows through wherever the surface of his life is touched by the wearing hand of life's frictions. He said about this experiment with the thirteen virtues, "As I knew or thought I knew what was right and wrong, I did not see why I might not always do the one and avoid the other."

The idea of acquiring virtue by deliberate practice did not evaporate with this one experiment. More than once in his letters we come across some reference to a treatise that he proposed to write on "The Art of Virtue." He evidently meant it to show the manner and means of practicing with the object of attaining each designated virtue. The booklet was never written, which is a pity for more reasons than one. Franklin wrote a letter about it to Lord Kames in 1760 that tells the story of the projected work.

"I purpose likewise a little work for the benefit of youth, to be called *The Art of Virtue.* From the title I think you will hardly conjecture what the nature of such a book may be. I must therefore explain it a little. Many people lead bad lives that would gladly lead good ones, but know not how to make the change. They have frequently *resolved* and *endeavoured* it; but in vain, because their endeavours have not been properly conducted. To expect people to be good, to be just, to be temperate &c., without *shewing* them *how* they should *become* so, seems like the ineffectual charity mentioned by the Apostle, which consisted in saying to the hungry, the cold, and the naked, 'Be ye fed, be ye warmed, be ye clothed,' without shewing them how they should get food, fire or clothing.

"Most people have naturally some virtues, but none have naturally *all* the virtues. To *acquire* those that are wanting and secure what we acquire as well as those we have naturally is the subject of *an art*. It is as properly an art as painting, navigation, or architecture; it is not enough that he is *advised* to be one, that he is *convinced* by the argument of his adviser, that it would be for his advantage to be one, and that he resolves to be one, but he must also be taught the principles of the art, be shown all the methods of working, and how to acquire the habits of using properly all the instruments; and thus regularly and gradually he arrives, by practice, at some perfection in the art. If he does not proceed thus, he is apt to meet with difficulties that discourage him, and make him drop the pursuit.

"My *Art of Virtue* has also its instruments, and teaches the manner of using them. Christians are directed to have faith in Christ, as the effectual means of obtaining the change they desire. It may, when sufficiently strong, be effectual with many; for a full opinion, that a Teacher is infinitely wise, good, and powerful, and that he will certainly reward and punish the obedient and disobedient, must give great weight to his precepts, and make them much more attended to by his disciples. But many have this faith in so weak a degree, that it does not produce the effect. Our *Art of Virtue* may, therefore, be of great service to those whose faith is unhappily not so strong, and may come in aid of its weakness. Such as are naturally well disposed, and have been so carefully educated, as that good habits have been early established, and bad ones prevented, have less need of this art; but all may be more or less benefited by it. It is, in short, to be adapted for universal use. I imagine what I have now been writing will seem to savour of great presumption: I must therefore speedily finish my little piece, and communicate the manuscript to you, that you may judge whether it is possible to make good such pretensions. I shall at the same time hope for the benefit of your corrections. I have, &c.

"B. FRANKLIN."

If Franklin had ever completed such a book and it was as useful as this sketch of it sounds, it might have competed with *Poor Richard's Almanack* or *The Way to Wealth,* in popularity.

The proposed book on the "Art of Virtue" was not Franklin's only venture in the field of religious authorship. He had a certain persistency that made it difficult for him to lay aside an idea even after it had proved to be not workable. He was always apparently of the opinion that public worship would be more popular if it were managed differently, and quite late in life when he was sixty-seven he ventured on an attempt to abridge the *Book of Common Prayer* of the Church of England.

He had a companion in the enterprise, Lord Le Despencer, formerly Sir Francis Dashwood.

Franklin's main contribution to this was the preface, which is especially interesting because of his frank expression of his attitude in regard to the details of public worship.[2] Franklin must

---

[2] *Cf.* Appendix.

have known perfectly the disinclination to make a change of this sort that is so characteristic of English churchmen, yet it is quite like him to enter into the revision, present his argument, and wait to see whether the effect would be favorable.

The arguments advanced in the preface will commend themselves to most modern minds, especially those for the omission of the reading of the imprecatory psalms and the abbreviation of the prayers for the visitation of the sick.

The venture did not meet with success. The book was printed but never gained much notice. Franklin says that "some were given away, very few sold, and I suppose the bulk became waste paper." In spite of this scant favor, one may well believe that Franklin did not in the least alter the convictions that he expresses in the preface.

Franklin was a reader of the Bible. He shows a decided familiarity with both the ideas and the words of the Scriptures, often quotes from them and always correctly. His comments on the spirit of the imprecatory psalms in comparison with that of the teachings of Jesus noted in the "Preface" would be sufficient indication of this. When one recalls the practical turn that his mind took in dealing with everything, whether in natural

Chriſt *Triumphing,*
A N D
Satan *Raging.*

A

SERMON

On Matth. XII. 28.

Wherein is proven, that the Kingdom of God
is come unto us at this Day.

First preached at *Nottingham* in *Penſilvania,*
Jan. 20. 1740,1.
And now publiſhed for the common
Benefit.

By *SAMUEL FINLEY,* Preacher of the Goſpel.

Aug. de bono perſev. in fine.

Ego --- cum per eos qui meos labores legunt, non
ſum doctior, verum etiam emendatior fio ; propitium
mihi Deum agnoſco : & hoc per Eccleſiæ Doctores
maxime expecto, ſi & in ipſorum manus veniunt, dig-
neturque noſſe quæ ſcribo.

Phil. I. 17. --- *Knowing that I am ſet for the Deſence
of the Goſpel.*

PHILADELPHIA:
Printed and Sold by B. FRANKLIN. 1741.

science or in spiritual affairs, it will not seem in the least irreverent in him that he once wrote an extra chapter [3] for the book of Genesis to emphasize his oft-expressed feelings on behalf of religious toleration. Of course he never seriously considered this as an effort to amend the Scriptures. He wrote this "fifty-first chapter" with no intention whatever of printing it for circulation but purely and simply for pleasure. Its clever imitation of Old Testament language and its appropriateness to New Testament teaching caused it to be sought after, so that it was put into print for private circulation. Later it was given wider currency. In a letter to William Strahan, Franklin says, "I was always unwilling to give a copy of this chapter for fear that it would be printed, and by that means I should be deprived of the pleasure I often had in amusing people with it." Mr. Strahan sent the "Parable" to the *London Chronicle* for April 14th to 17th, 1764, in connection with which he wrote, "Some time ago, being in company with a friend from North America, as well known throughout Europe for his ingenious discoveries in natural philosophy, as to

---

[3] There is some doubt as to whether Franklin really originated this chapter. He was, in fact, once accused of plagiarism in connection with it. His frequent use of it, however, gave currency to the belief that he was the author.

his country-men for his sagacity, his usefulness, and activity, in every public spirited measure, and to his acquaintance for all social virtues; the conversation happened to turn on the subject of persecutions. My friend, whose understanding is as enlarged as his heart is benevolent, did not fail to urge many unanswerable arguments against a practice so obviously repugnant to every dictate of humanity. At length, in support of what he advanced, he called for a Bible and turning to the Book of Genesis read as follows:

1. And it came to pass after these things, that Abraham sat in the door of his tent, about the going down of the sun:

2. And behold a man, bowed with age, came from the way of the wilderness, leaning on a staff.

3. And Abraham arose and met him, and said unto him, Turn in, I pray thee, and wash thy feet, and tarry all night, and thou shalt arise early on the morrow, and go on thy way.

4. But the man said, Nay, for I will abide under this tree.

5. And Abraham pressed him greatly, so he turned, and they went into the tent, and Abraham baked unleavened bread, and they did eat.

6. And when Abraham saw that the man

blessed not God, he said unto him, Wherefore dost thou not worship the most high God, creator of heaven and earth?

7. And the man answered and said, I do not worship the God thou speakest of, neither do I call upon his name; for I have made to myself a God, which abideth alway in mine house, and provideth me with all things.

8. And Abraham's zeal was kindled against the man, and he arose and drove him forth with blows into the wilderness.

9. And at midnight God called unto Abraham saying, Abraham, where is the stranger?

10. And Abraham answered and said, Lord he would not worship thee, neither would he call upon thy name, therefore have I driven him out from before my face into the wilderness.

11. And God said, Have I borne with him these hundred ninety and eight years, and nourished him, and cloathed him, notwithstanding his rebellion against me; and couldst not thou, that are thy self a sinner, beare with him one night!

12. And Abraham said, Let not the anger of my Lord wax hot against his servant; lo, I have sinned, forgive me, I pray thee.

13. And Abraham arose, and went forth into the wilderness, and sought diligently for the man,

and found him, and returned with him to the tent, and when he had entreated him kindly, he sent him away on the morrow with gifts.

14. And God spake again unto Abraham, saying For this thy sin shall thy seed be afflicted four hundred years in a strange land:

15. But for thy repentance will I deliver them, and they shall come forth with power, and with gladness of heart, and with much substance.

"I own I was struck with the aptness of the passage to the subject, and did not fail to express my surprise, that in all the discourses I had read against a practice so diametrically opposite to the genuine spirit of an holy religion, I did not remember to have seen this chapter quoted; nor did I recollect my ever having read it, tho' no stranger to my Bible. Next morning, turning to the Book of Genesis, I found that there was no chapter, and that the whole was a well meant invention of my friend, whose sallies of humor, in which he is a great master, have always a useful and benevolent tendency."

Sometimes Franklin read it from a leaflet inserted in his own Bible, and sometimes, as on this occasion with Strahan, recited it from memory. The whole pious hoax is characteristic of Franklin's humor and at the same time gives a hint of his familiarity with the Bible.

As has been said there is doubt as to whether or not Franklin really wrote this fifty-first chapter of Genesis, but there is no doubt that he did attempt similar things. His "Proposed New Version of the Bible" can scarcely be considered a serious bit of writing for it was undoubtedly a shrewd satire upon the ways and spirit of regal governments and the Bible was used merely as a vehicle.[4] "It seems almost incredible," says Smyth, "that the point of this prodigious satire should have been missed by any thoughtful reader; yet true it is that one of the most sagacious of recent critics and one of the most learned of living historians has been completely deceived by it."

Matthew Arnold commented upon it. "I remember the relief with which, after long feeling the sway of Franklin's imperturbable common sense, I came upon a project of his for a new version of the Book of Job, to replace the old version, the style of which, says Franklin, has become obsolete and thence less agreeable. 'I give,' he continues, 'a few verses, which may serve as a sample of the kind of version I would recommend.' We all recollect the famous verse in our translation:

---

[4] *Cf.* Appendix.

'Then Satan answered the Lord, and said, Doth Job fear God for naught?' Franklin makes this, 'Does your Majesty imagine that Job's conduct is the effect of mere personal attachment and affection?' I well remember how when I first read that I drew a deep breath of relief, and said to myself after all, there is a stretch of humanity beyond Franklin's victorious good sense."

There is another "parable" that Franklin either wrote or used, to illustrate the need of brotherly love. It is a purported incident in the lives of the brothers Reuben, Simeon, Levi, and Judah.

There is, however, a piece of Franklin's writing on the Bible that is neither a veiled satire nor a clever bit of writing to convey a moral lesson. The connection in which it first appeared is somewhat uncertain. One suspects that the impulse that gave rise to it came at about the time that he was interested in the abridgment of the English Book of Common Prayer. It is a proposed new version of the Lord's Prayer.[5] One is not very much impressed by the supposed improvement, and not much more by the "Reasons for the Change of Expression." It is noteworthy, however, as showing the interest that Frank-

---

[5] *Cf.* Appendix.

lin had in the wording of familiar Scripture.

In spite of the undoubted sincerity of Franklin's beliefs, such as they were, one could hardly claim reverence as one of his characteristics. He had a perfectly amazing curiosity which accounts for his scientific interest and success, and he had also, what often goes with such a power of curiosity, the desire to make changes and improvements. Possibly we should not say that his general mental attitude was irreverent, for that would be not quite true. We should say rather that he did not have that reverence for things as they have been, that so many men, particularly Englishmen of a certain type, have been noted for. Franklin was a Democrat to the core. He did not believe in the sanctities of the monarchical régime. All purely human institutions were to him open to reëxamination. If they could not stand the light of pure reason he did not hesitate to suggest their alteration.

As we have seen, he did believe in prayer, but as he had not hesitated to discard the prayers of others and make prayers for himself, so apparently, he did not hesitate to retranslate or recast even the Lord's Prayer, if by putting it in more vernacular language it would seem to become more useful. This is all the more interesting when we consider that not for a long time after his day did the subject of vernacular translations of the Scriptures come to the fore as they have since the beginning of our present century.

The most serious blot on Franklin's escutcheon has been that he apparently openly accepted into his family circle an illegitimate son, William Franklin. What has made it appear even more morally callous is that it has seemed as though his wife Deborah had acquiesced in it. If these were the facts, that Franklin had a natural son by some unknown mother, and that Deborah Reed accepted the child and brought him up with her own it would warrant some of the unsparing criticism that has been visited on the Franklin household. But Franklin was never morally callous. Such letters as he wrote could not come from so gross and insensible a moral nature as some of his critics have attributed to him. And absolutely the last thing that any critic could make stick on Franklin is the charge of hypocrisy.

Hitherto the kindest thing that one could do was to pass it over as one of the things that might not have seemed so serious a few generations ago. Though there never has been a time when such a thing was not a serious commentary on a man's character.

However, we do not have to be so uncertain about the matter any longer. The recent finding of several hitherto unknown letters gives conclusive evidence that the mother of William was none other than Deborah Reed—Mrs. Deborah Reed Rogers, whom Franklin took to wife September 1, 1730.

One of the most convincing letters chronologically is one that Benjamin Franklin wrote to his mother dated April 12, 1750, in which he says: "as to your grandchildren, Will is now nineteen years of age," and then goes on to speak of Sally. This would make the year of William's birth in 1731 on some date previous to April 12 of that year and by that much subsequent to his taking Deborah Reed to wife on September 1, 1730.

Before coming to any conclusion however, we should ask more conclusive evidence than this. Such evidence has been compiled by Charles Henry Hart in a recent pamphlet, "Who Was the Mother of Franklin's Son?" The gist of the argument is this:

Franklin had an affection for Deborah Reed very shortly after his arrival at Philadelphia. The youth of both of them made marriage unadvisable at that time. Franklin was absent in England from December 24, 1724, to October

11, 1726, almost two years. During his absence Deborah Reed had married "one Rogers, a potter," with whom "she was never happy and soon parted from him, refusing to co-habit with him or bear his name it being said that he had another wife." This Rogers was a worthless sort who got into debt and ran away, in 1727 or 1728, to the West Indies and died there.

The affection between Franklin and Deborah Reed renewed, but now there were other difficulties in the way. Deborah's marriage to Rogers was not valid if it were sure that he had another wife living in England. On account of the distance, etc., this could not be proved. There were the debts which his successor might be called upon to pay. "We ventured however," says the autobiography, "over all these difficulties and I took her to wife, September 1, 1730. None of the inconveniences happened that we had apprehended; she proved a good and faithful helpmate, assisted me much by attending the shop; we throve together and have ever mutually endeavor'd to make each other happy. Thus I corrected that great *Erratum* as well as I could." Franklin did not use words without full accuracy, he was a master of language. He did not say they were married. It is probable that no marriage cere-

mony was performed, but in view of the legal
difficulties they agreed to live together as man
and wife until time and their good characters
should make them one in the eyes of the law.

William Franklin was born just about the time
that Benjamin and Deborah joined their fortunes.
On July 3, 1812, he writes "my health, considering I am in my eighty-second year, is generally
good." That would put his birthday some time
in 1730 or 1731.

More conclusive than chronology is the fact
that Deborah speaks of him as her son. There
are not many autograph letters of hers but we
have one such written December 24, 1751, to
William Strahan in which she says, "My son is
gone to Boston on a visit to his friends." And
Strahan in 1758 wrote her. "Your son I really
think one of the prettiest young gentleman seen
here (London) from America." As Mr. Hart
says: "can it be imagined or conceived that any
wife would call her husband's illegitimate child
by another woman, 'my son,' or would an intimate
friend and correspondent of the family compli-
ment her upon her husband's child?"

In another letter Franklin refers to Deborah's
mother, Mrs. Reed, as Billy's grandmother. And
Sarah Franklin refers to William as her brother,

while her letters evidence the warmest sisterly affection for him.

The facts would seem to be pretty plain that Benjamin Franklin and Deborah Reed wanted to live together, and because of the legal tangle she was in they could not be formally married so they did exactly what one would have expected Benjamin Franklin to have done in such situation, the most common sense thing. And furthermore it does not seem to have affected either the tenderest relations with his family nor his good reputation in the city where he lived. If there had been anything very disreputable about his family affairs there were plenty of political opponents of Franklin's who would not have been slow to make use of it.

If our reasoning has been correct from this data, so much of which has only recently come to light, and some of it even yet unpublished, the blot on Franklin's escutcheon was not a blot but rather a shadow which a clearer light largely removes. When once a tale becomes popularly known and is handed down as a tradition, there is little likelihood that it will be very quickly changed. It can be changed, however, and it is to be hoped that Franklin's good name and that of his wife and son William will some day be freed

THE
ART
OF
PREACHING,

IN IMITATION OF

HORACE's
ART OF POETRY.

LONDON, Printed:
PHILADELPHIA: Re-printed, and
Sold by B. FRANKLIN, in *Market-Street.*

M,DCC,XLI,

from the shadow that has so unjustly rested on it.

Morals are high or low by comparison with the average of the times in which a man lives. In England in the eighteenth century, especially the first half of it, the average was at an exceedingly low point. The king openly kept his mistresses and the Duke of Grafton, who became prime minister, was in the habit of appearing with his mistress at the theater. Drunkenness and foul talk were not considered any particular discredit to Walpole. Nor did his flagrant conduct of the government by bribery and corruption of all sorts bring down open condemnation upon his head. Ladies of high rank swore prodigiously in public places.

Fidelity to the marriage vows was sneered out of fashion. Adultery, especially in the upper classes, was a sport in which the wronged husband got the laugh. Lord Chesterfield in his letters to his son instructs him in the art of seduction as part of a polite education.

"At the other end of the social scale," says Green, "lay the masses of the poor. They were ignorant and brutal to a degree which it is hard to conceive, for the vast increase of the population which followed on the growth of towns and the development of manufactures had been met by no effort for their religious or educational improvement. Not a new parish had been created. Hardly a single new church had been built. Schools there were none, save the grammar schools of Edward and Elizabeth. The rural peasantry, who were fast being reduced to pauperism by the abuse of the poor-laws, were left without moral or religious training of any sort. 'We saw but one Bible in the parish of Cheddar,' said Hannah More at a far later time, 'and that was used to prop a flowerpot.' "

Possibly it is not fair to judge any age by its vices, for humanity has blackened itself in every century. It is nearer the point to examine the stable institutions, the courts of justice, and the Church. And here we do not find much to brighten the picture. It is incredible to us that such ferocious laws should have disgraced the books. When Franklin was in England, lads were hung for petty larceny, and women were liable to be publicly flogged or to be burned at the stake for minor offenses. Temple Bar was adorned with a constantly renewed exhibition of human heads.

The laws in the American Colonies were not quite so severe but Franklin's day at home was that of the pillory and the whipping post. Runaways were nailed by the ears to door posts and, when their number of hours were up, released by slitting their ears.

The severity of the laws in England reflects the terror of society at the unrestrained lawlessness of the time. The criminal classes were bold and ruthless. There was no effective police, and mobs in London and elsewhere, when once started, burned, and pillaged almost at will.

The England that Franklin visited in his youth was devoid of vital religion except in some groups in the middle class. In the higher circles, "every one laughs," said Montesquieu on his visit to England, "if one talks of religion." The prominent statesmen were for the most part unbelievers in any form of Christianity. Thackeray was not a historian but a satirist and as such his description must be assessed, but an age must be pretty far gone when anything like Selwyn's chaplain could have been tolerated.

This worthy clergyman takes care to tell us that he does not believe in his religion, though, thank Heaven, he is not so great a rogue as a lawyer. He goes on Mr. Selwyn's errands, any errands, and is proud, he says, to be that gentleman's proveditor. He waits upon the Duke of

Queensberry—"old Q"—and exchanges petty stories with that aristocrat. He comes home "after a hard day's christening," as he says, and writes to his patron after sitting down to whist and partridges for supper. He revels in thoughts of oxcheek and burgundy—he is a boistrous, uproarious parasite, licks his master's shoes with explosions of laughter and with cunning smack and gusto, and likes the taste of that blacking as much as the best claret in old Q's cellar. He has "Rabelais" and "Horace" at his greasy finger ends. He is inexpressibly mean and curiously jolly; kindly and good natured in secret—a tender hearted knave, not a venomous lickspittle.

Every age has the kind of religious teachers and leaders that it wants. This was the age of Deism, and Deism of any sort is morally impotent. A religion that is exhausted of its supernatural content has no power over the human conscience. A religion of this type served by such ministers naturally bred an ignoble society. If men believe that Christianity is not true but that it is useful they are on the way to lose their moral vigor totally. A feature of this age in the church was its dread of enthusiasm. Even Bishop Butler, who with Berkeley and William Law were among its bright lights, forbade Whitefield and the Wesleys to preach in his parish.

A brighter day for religion was about to dawn. With the coming of the Wesleyan revival, English and Colonial religious life was to rise to higher levels than it had ever yet known, and was to produce a society of purer standards than any hitherto attained on either side of the Atlantic.

It was while these conditions were at their lowest ebb that Franklin came upon the scene. His early Puritan training was an inheritance that left him unusually well fortified in morals. It is remarkable that a youth so lively and vital should have been plunged into English life at such a time and emerged with so little stain upon him.

The irregularity of Franklin's family was not carried out in callous indifference to the moral standards of his day. On the contrary, his acknowledging William and his taking Deborah Reed to wife seem to be part of an honorable attempt to right what he considered an *erratum* in an age when it would have been accepted if he had considered both of them as incidents to be quickly passed by and forgotten.

Happily there is no need to change the tradition which is far more important, that Benjamin Franklin all his active life was a benefactor of humanity. Here we enter an undisputed field. Measured by quantity or by quality there is no man, not excepting George Washington, who contributed more to the advancement of material prosperity, right thinking, and political righteousness than did Franklin in those acutely formative years of the American republic.

The early years of Franklin's life in Philadelphia were spent in a diligent effort to acquire a competence. During those years of work and saving he made himself a master printer and acquired the reputation of being a good citizen. He did not a little public printing and many of those contracts must have been profitable. There has never been brought to light any irregularities in his business dealings nor do any of his contemporaries accuse him of any sharp dealing. That he was a good trader there can be little doubt, and we are even more sure that he kept close and methodical account of his transactions. His financial records have survived to an astonishing degree and are open to inspection.

He does not seem to have been avaricious but on the contrary appears to have had always in mind his own early struggles, and to be ready to set up in business any of his own men who were worthy of the venture.

While yet a young man, he became a leader in many public affairs in the city of Philadelphia and the province of Pennsylvania. Indeed with the progress of his fortunes he increasingly gave his energies to matters of public service. The making of money as such did not seem to interest him, and as soon as he was able he disentangled himself from business and devoted himself to the two things that most interested him, public affairs and scientific investigation. The number of things that he dipped into is simply incredible. He established a fire department for the city and installed street-cleaning devices. He invented his famous Franklin stove which marks the beginning of modern heating devices. He did not appear to desire profit from his scientific work but worked on such things for the pure love of it. In regard to the Franklin stove he refused to take out any patents on the ground that as we all receive so much benefit from the inventions of others it is only right and just that we should contribute to their well-being.

A surprisingly large number of Franklin's projects, nearly all of them, in fact, have continued to exist and to be useful to this present day. This is after all not so surprising when we consider the singular type of mind that he possessed. He was free from prejudice, and from the cramping hand of convention. He was a scientist in the art of living as well as with his devices. Given a man who has the thirst for facts and is not warped by precedent, you would expect to find just the type of position that he held in religion. He was rational, but was not a rationalist because he had that matchless instinct for telling just the moment where reason stops and where sentiment, faith, or guesswork must begin. But to return to some of his enduring projects.

The *Pennsylvania Gazette* which he established in 1728 is in existence to-day as the *Saturday Evening Post*. In 1731, as a result of the Junto, he established the Library Company of Philadelphia. It was the first subscription library in North America and is to-day one of the most conspicuously useful libraries in the city of Philadelphia.

The Charity School of Philadelphia was founded in 1740. Franklin wrote "Hints for the Consideration Respecting the Orphan School House in Philadelphia" and in 1743 his first proposal for a complete education of youth was mentioned. In 1748 he wrote and printed his "Proposal Relating to the Education of Youth in Pennsylvania," which led to the formation of the college which is now the University of Pennsylvania. He was chosen president of the Board of Trustees and remained a member of the board for more than forty years.

It was on his initiation through a pamphlet published by him in 1743 that the American Philosophical Society was founded somewhat later. This organization is still flourishing and makes frequent contributions of value in its field.

In 1751, with Dr. Thomas Bond and others, he promoted the founding of the Pennsylvania Hospital, the first of its kind in America and still in successful operation.

In 1752 with other business men he aided in establishing "The Philadelphia Contributionship for the Insurance of Houses from Loss by Fire." This is a mutual fire insurance company still in prosperous existence.

He established a regular system for setting up in the printing business such of his journeymen as were capable, and at the end of six years they became independent of him if they proved competent. He served as clerk of the Provisional Assembly and was foremost in efforts to smooth the rough pathway of the citizens whose interests were in constant conflict with the governor sent out from England. He lent his own personal credit for the proper equipping of Braddock's expedition, a public service for which he got no thanks and which cost him dearly. If we add to this his contribution to our knowledge of electricity, the invention of lightning rods, and many other such things, the list becomes formidable indeed.

Permanent and useful as all these things are, they are inconsiderable in comparison with the contribution that he made to the establishing of our free republic. It is conceivable that the Colonies might have gained their freedom without Franklin, just as the new world might have been discovered without Columbus or the Hebrews have escaped from Egypt without Moses. But it is equally evident that without Franklin the story would have been very different. Indeed it is difficult for one to see how the colonies could have won their freedom if Franklin had not been "raised up," as our fathers used to say, for just such a day. General Washington had the military skill, the character, and the disposition to insure adequate leadership on this side of the Atlantic. But half of the issue lay in the proper handling of events on the other side, and here is where Franklin made his great contribution to American freedom. In all, he spent, during three periods of service, nearly twenty-five years on the other side of the Atlantic, sixteen years in his two missions to England preceding the Declaration of Independence, and about nine in France during and after the eight years of the war of the Colonies against England.

It was in France that he reached the height of his powers, and it was there that the magnitude of his character was most widely appreciated. The self-possessed calmness, the wit, the natural gayety, the scientific achievements, and the almost unbelievable capacity for capably meeting every situation that arose, made Franklin, for nearly a decade, the most celebrated man in France.

By his diplomatic skill he was able to obtain from the almost bankrupt treasury of France credits to the extent of more than twenty millions of francs, and enough men, munitions, and ships to prolong the struggle until Britain was prepared to accede to the terms that were to make the Colonies a free and independent nation. His was the mind, too, that engineered that terrible and swift war of privateers on English shipping, which has left us the shining name of John Paul Jones as a dashing fighter.

After the surrender at Yorktown, Franklin's duties were not done. A treaty of peace had to be framed and signed that would be satisfactory not only to the Colonies but to England and France as well. He was seventy-five years old when appointed to negotiate that treaty, and seventy-nine when at last Congress accepted his resignation as minister to France.

Some men are unable to do serious things except in a serious and ponderous manner. Franklin carried, all those years in France, burdens that seemed to be all out of proportion to any man's endurance, yet he exhibited complacency, gayety, and humor in his social life. It disturbed the somber Adams and infuriated the impatient Lee, but it invariably, in the expressive idiom of our contemporaries, "brought home the bacon."

Such serenity and unfailing perseverance are not wholly temperamental. Temperament cannot endure for such a term of years as Franklin gave his country during his service in France. Character, vision, belief, convictions, whatever we may prefer to call that inner fiber of the soul, alone can provide the rock foundation to withstand such a prolonged conflict.

A
LETTER

From the Reverend

Mr. WHITEFIELD

To a Friend in *LONDON,*

Shewing the Fundamental Error of the Book,
Entitled, The Whole DUTY of MAN.

PHILADELPHIA:
Printed and Sold by B. Franklin,
M,DCC,XL.

Franklin's deepest feelings of a religious nature during this period find expression in more than one of his letters but notably in this one to William Strahan:

Passy, August 19, 1784.

. . . But after all, my dear friend, do not imagine that I am vain enough to ascribe our success to any superiority in any of those points. I am too well acquainted with all the springs and levers of our machine not to see that our human means were unequal to our undertaking, and that, if it had not been for the justice of our cause, and the consequent interposition of Providence, in which we had faith, we must have been ruined. If I had ever before been an atheist, I should now have been convinced of the being and government of a Deity! It is he who abases the proud and favours the humble. May we never forget his goodness to us, and may our future conduct manifest our gratitude.

One can read Franklin's letters by the score, treating of every conceivable situation and problem, and nowhere will one find the note of complaint or of lack of hope. On the contrary, while never foolishly shutting his eyes to the dangers and perplexities of his personal tasks and those of his beloved Colonies, he continually shows the most tranquil and cheerful attitude of mind.

This, as we have previously said, was not entirely tempermental but was the result of his definitely chosen frame of mind—a mind not very far, if we may say so, from that advocated in the New Testament. He had faith in his fellow human beings, and faith in the kindly intent of God as the Father of men towards his children.

There is, in the collection of Franklin writings kept by the Shipley family, a letter-press copy of an editorial, evidently written by him and intended for publication in the *Pennsylvania Gazette,* that gives a good idea of the workings of his mind in this direction:

THE INTERNAL STATE OF AMERICA

BEING A TRUE DESCRIPTION OF THE INTEREST AND POLICY OF THAT VAST CONTINENT

There is a tradition, that, in the planting of New England, the first settlers met with many difficulties and hardships as is generally the case when a civilized people attempt establishing themselves in a wilderness country. Being piously dispos'd, they sought relief from Heaven, by laying their wants and distresses before the Lord, in frequent set days of fasting and prayer. Constant meditation and discourse on these subjects kept their minds gloomy and discontented; and, like the children of Israel, there were many dispos'd to return to that Egypt, which persecution had induc'd them to abandon. At length, when it was proposed in the Assembly to proclaim another fast, a farmer of plain sense rose, and remark'd, that the inconveniences they suffer'd, and concerning which they had so often weary'd Heaven with their complaints, were not so great as they might have expected, and were diminishing every day, as the Colony strengthen'd; that the earth began to reward their labor, and to furnish liberally for their subsistence; that the seas and rivers were full of fish, the air sweet, the climate healthy; and, above all, that they were there in the full enjoyment of liberty, civil and religious. He therefore thought, that reflecting and conversing on these subjects would be more comfortable, as tending more to make them contented with their situation; and that it would be more becoming the gratitude they ow'd to the Divine Being, if, instead of a fast, they should proclaim a Thanksgiving. His Advice was taken; and from that day to this they have, in every Year, observ'd circumstances of public felicity sufficient to furnish employment for a Thanksgiving Day; which is therefore constantly ordered and religiously observed. . . .

In Franklin's later years he did not hesitate to give expression to similar feelings on various public occasions, as in his reply to the address to him of the Assembly of Pennsylvania, of which he was elected president immediately on his return from France in 1785. After thanking the Assembly for the friendly approbation that they had expressed, he said: "I hope the peace with which God has been graciously pleased to bless us may be lasting, and that the free Constitution we now enjoy may long contribute to promote our common felicity."

None of these public avowals of genuine faith in God surpasses that which he made in 1787 at the Constitutional Convention, of which he was a member. During one of the earlier meetings he moved that the sessions be begun with prayer, and in the speech in support of his motion he said: "The longer I live, the more convincing proofs I see of this truth, *that God governs in the Affairs of man.* And if a sparrow cannot fall to the ground without his notice, is it probable that an empire can rise without his aid? We have been assured, Sir, in the Sacred Writings, that 'except the Lord build the house, they labour in vain that build it!' I firmly believe this; and I also believe, that without his concurring aid, we shall succeed in this political building no better than the builders of Babel."

Along with this devout acknowledgment of God's activity in the affairs of men, is the same delicious humor over the self-deception and vagaries of some alleged religious persons, as appears in this letter to his cousin Jonathan written shortly before his return from France in 1785:

I received your letter of December 16th, relating to Jonas Hartwell. I had before written to our minister at Madrid, Mr. Carmichael, requesting him to apply for the release of that man. Enclosed I send his answer, with copies of other papers relating to the affair. The simpleton will be discharged, perhaps after being a little whipped for his folly, and that may not be amiss. We have here another New England man, Thayer, formerly a candidate for the ministry, who converted himself lately at Rome, and is now preparing a return home for the purpose of converting his countrymen. Our ancestors from Catholic became first Church-of-England men, and then refined into Presbyterians. To change now from Presbyterianism to Popery seems to me refining backwards, from white sugar to brown.

It would be useless to argue that Benjamin Franklin was a religious man in the sense that the average person uses that phrase. He most certainly espoused no dogma, nor made any professions, nor vows, and he was in no sense a propagandist of even those convictions and that faith in God which he had, though he was ever ready to avow them.

If we are to judge his life by the latter half of the great commandment—"Thou shalt love the Lord, thy God, with all thy heart and thy neighbor as thyself"—Franklin would deserve a verdict distinctly favorable. The first half of his life was spent in acquiring independence and leisure. Thereafter he gave himself unstintedly not for the sake of honors or emoluments, but for the good of his fellow men. He worked for the enrichment of humanity through his scientific pursuits, and even more he labored for the establishment of a free and democratic government where men should have greater opportunities for advancement than they had ever previously known.

One cannot help but feel that if men were really to measure religious values as it is written that they gauge in heaven—"by their fruits"—Franklin would rank higher than many a scholastic and dogmatist. This is not only the sentiment of a late generation. His own generation was generous in appreciation of Franklin's life, and his service to its welfare. Few men could have deserved or received more gratifying appreciation than is shown in this paragraph of a letter to him from George Washington.

If to be venerated for benevolence, if to be admired for talents, if to be esteemed for patriotism, if to be beloved for philanthropy, can gratify human mind, you must not have lived in vain.   And I flatter myself that it will not be ranked among the least grateful occurrences of your life to be assured that so long as I retain my memory you will be recollected with respect, reveration and affection by your friend.

The fruit of a truly unselfish life is an inner feeling that the cynic can never understand.   One may be conscious of one's failure to attain ideals, and mindful of repeated defeats, yet, overtopping all disappointments, there is a deep, inner satisfaction in having fought the fight, finished the course and won the prize of life's real value that will eternally endure.

Franklin was past eighty when he wrote the concluding part of his autobiography, and one feels that he must have penned these sentences that occur in the opening part of it, a sort of preface, last of all:

If it were left to my choice, I should have no

objection to go over the same life from its beginning to its end. Requesting only the advantage authors have of correcting in a second edition the faults of the first. So I would also wish to change some incidents for others more favorable. Notwithstanding, if this condition were denied, I should still accept the offer, recommending the same life.

Another evidence that Franklin's religion was of the definite and practical type of the Good Samaritan was that his mind was never easy or satisfied when roaming about amid the uncertainties of speculation but always logical and direct when occupied with definite and specific good to mankind.

He nowhere indulges in attempts to prove the existence of God. He assumes God as the guiding hand in all human affairs and concerns himself with intelligent effort to accomplish what he thinks is God's good intent for men. Such emphasis leads invariably to the problem of education of the younger generation. Next to his service in helping to make the United States government a possibility, Franklin's greatest contribution to the spiritual life of the nation was possibly the impetus that he gave to education.

In 1749, as we have already mentioned, he wrote, printed and circulated "Proposals Relating to the Education of Youth in Pennsylvania," which led to the formation of the academy that in the course of time developed into the University of Pennsylvania, the first institution in North America to be granted a university charter. Its subsequent history amply justifies the broad and devout wisdom of its founder, for it has given to the nation a generous stream of educators, clergymen, scientists, jurists, physicians, and others of like serviceable disposition.

A man's educational beliefs are his best creed, for in them he must necessarily indicate his real philosophy of life. A Study of the "Proposals" would be refreshing to the modern educator, and the atmosphere of many an institution would benefit by holding to what Franklin believed to be the real end of learning. The modernist in education would be surprised and delighted at what Franklin says about teaching the sciences and languages, especially about the study and mastery of one's native tongue. After giving an outline of what he considered ought to be taught, the outline goes on to state "with the whole should be constantly inculcated and cultivated, that *benignity of mind,* which shows itself in *searching* for and *seizing true merits,* should also be often presented to youth, explained and impressed on their minds, as consisting in an *inclination* joined with an ability to serve mankind, one's country, friends and family; which ability is (with the blessing of God) to be acquired or greatly increased by true learning; and should indeed be the great *aim* and *end* of all learning."

Throughout this pamphlet on education, Franklin makes liberal uses of footnotes in which he quotes from various leaders of thought—some of them well known, others less so in our time, including Milton, Locke, Hutcheson, Rollin, and others. Sometimes the footnote is an excursus of his own. These footnotes are illuminating as to the convictions of Franklin's own mind. "To have in view the *glory* and *service of God,* as some express themselves, is only the same thing in other words. *For doing good* to men is the only *service to God* in our power; and to *imitate his beneficences* is to *glorify him.* Hence *Milton* says 'The *end* of learning is to repair the ruins of our first parents, by regaining to *know God aright,* and out of that knowledge to *love him,* to imitate him, and to be *like him,* as we may be nearest by possessing our souls of pure virtue.' The others quoted express themselves in the same tenor, viz. that education is primarily for the production of character. . . ."

Franklin concludes the pamphlet by quoting again: "Whatever else one may have learned, if he comes into the world from his schooling and masters, quite unacquainted with the nature, rank and condition of mankind, and the *duties of human life* (in its more ordinary circumstances at least) he hath lost his time; *he is not educated;* he is not prepared for the world; he is not qualified for society; he is not fitted for discharging the *proper business of man.* The way therefore to judge whether education be on a right footing or not is to compare it with the end; or to consider what it does in order to accomplish youth for choosing or *behaving well* in the various conditions, relations and incidents of life."

Franklin and the Board of Trustees that he gathered around him really tried to carry out these aims in the conduct of the academy. His correspondence with the Rev. Samuel Johnson of New England, whom he was at one time anxious to secure as its Rector, indicates a genuine devotion to these ideals. The generous way in which Franklin sacrificed his personal preferences for a leisurely life of philosophical study, at the call of public duty and demand, is a practical demonstration that he himself placed the "doing of good to men the only service of God in our power" ahead of his personal wish for a more comfortable life.

Better even than his educational ideals was the intelligent sympathy with young persons in the process of education, which Franklin's correspondence indicates. He was so beautifully human and affectionate that all his letters of advice to them are free from preachiness, yet at the same time full of sound moral advice. While he was living in France he had occasion to write to Master E. N. Bancroft, then a young lad at school in England, who was in a collateral line of the Bancrofts who gave us the famous historian. In this letter he refers to two letters previously received from the lad. He must have been a boy of considerable character or he would not have been found writing to an old man of seventy-eight who was Ambassador to France. Franklin's letter [6] to the lad is a gem; one paragraph might with profit be hung on the wall of every boys' school. "Pursue your studies diligently; they may qualify you to act in some honorable station hereafter, and distinguish you from the ignorant vulgar. Strive to be one of the best boys among

[6] From an unpublished letter.

A
SERMON
ON THE
Important Doctrine
OF
REGENERATION.

Preached at *Grace Church-Street*, the *Sixth* of
the *Third* Month, 1688.

By WILLIAM DEWSBURY.

Taken from his Mouth in Short-hand.

William Dewſbury *was one of the firſt Preachers
among thoſe called* Quakers; *a very zealous
Teacher and an eminent Inſtrument to the Conver-
ſion of many.* Sewel's Hiſtory, page 591.

PHILADELPHIA:

Reprinted and Sold by B. FRANKLIN,
in *Market-Street.* M,DCC,XLI.

your acquaintance; 'tis the road that leads to the character of a good man." He continues: "Be dutiful and affectionate to your good mother, particularly now in the absence of your father, which will draw down upon you the blessings of God, and procure you the regard of all your father's friends, and of every one that knows your family."

The record of Master Bancroft would indicate that the counsel of the aged Ambassador was taken in good earnest, for the boy in later life became an eminent physician and rendered distinguished service with the British army.

It would be, as we have seen, a hopeless task to endeavor to show that Benjamin Franklin was in the conventional sense a religious man; for this he distinctly was not. He was conventional in nothing. Franklin was in nearly every phase of his mental and spiritual life far in advance of the conventional limits of his contemporaries. But it is not at all a hopeless task, as we trust this collection of his expressed thoughts shows, to demonstrate that the consciousness of the presence of God in human affairs played a decisive part in his personal life and in the decisions that he was called upon to make regarding the public affairs that were intrusted to him and in the shaping of which he had so large a share.

The progress of religion since Franklin's day has been steadily in the direction that he himself took, namely, toward the practical application of the consciousness of God to personal and public affairs, and there has been an equally steady recession in the feeling of the importance of theoretical and speculative religious opinions.

Orthodoxy has been always the term applied to opinions held on the speculative side of religion. In modern Christian history the orthodox man has been the man whose opinions as to the nature of the inspiration of the Scriptures, the person of Christ, and the way in which men are saved by the death of Christ were such as were agreed to by the historic and contemporary thought of the church. The unorthodox man, no matter what his personal conduct may have been, even though it squared nicely with the Sermon on the Mount and the thirteenth chapter of First Corinthians, was a heretic, because his opinions were wrong. It has not mattered that such a man really believed in God, and really believed in and practiced prayer. He was nevertheless a heretic. We shall have to admit that according to conventional standards Franklin was undeniably a heretic. He did believe in God and pray to him. He did act on that belief and was apparently bettered by that prayer, but he had little or nothing to say about the inspiration of the Scriptures and was not at all clear as to the personality of Jesus. It is fortunate for him that he did not live in France three centuries earlier. He would have been a fair mark for the inquisition.

But on the other, the human side of religion, the side that is concerned with doing good to others, his conduct, and his method of using his life were triumphantly Christian. His virtues were those of the Good Samaritan; his was the good will that vaunteth not itself, is not puffed up, beareth all things, believeth all things, hopeth all things, and endureth all things.

Love, it is written, never faileth. In those fearful days in France, when the impossible was asked of him by the Continental Government, and when he was being pestered, lied about, thwarted, and damaged in countless ways by some of his American associates, Franklin could never have come through successfully if he had not possessed that quality that "never faileth." He did manifestly bear good will to his fellow men and was ready to sacrifice himself for them.

We must not forget that the public service Franklin rendered the Colonies during all these strenuous years was a personal sacrifice. He was a rich man. After he passed the age of forty-two he effected a retirement from business and thereafter was in receipt of an income, and free to come and go as he chose. He never subsequently devoted himself at all to making money; he had enough for his purposes. Moreover, he had interests that fascinated and absorbed him. He could, by following up his philosophical and scientific studies, get all the personal satisfaction and fame that a man could wish for. Furthermore, the work that he would be doing would be of infinite worth to the prosperity of mankind. His inventions were almost uniformly useful and promised to be more so. It requires no great imagination to fancy what his labors would have accomplished in the field of electricity. Yet he spent nearly all his best days in the effort to compose human quarrels and in struggling to wrest something like order, peace, and justice out of a quarrelsome and peace-denying age. Here again his vision was not wrong, because peace and justice are more important for mankind than mechanical inventions, but men of dull spiritual vision cannot easily see this. Are we then justified in the feeling that this rich man, with fascinating and useful work at his hand, exhibited the foremost of the Christian virtues—the denial of self?

It seems to us as we read his letters that few men in the annals of modern history have so voluntarily and generously laid down their own lives that others might be benefited.

Throughout his life his burdens were heavy and his anxieties were often distressing, for he suffered much opposition. He retained, however, a cheerful temper, being habitually kindly and tolerant. He had a talent for happiness. He told Nicholas Collin that all the griefs and sufferings of the world are but as the momentary pricking of a pin in comparison with the total happiness of our existence.

During Franklin's lifetime there was rising gradually but steadily the tide of sentiment against human slavery. After a life spent mostly in the service of human liberty it is not surprising that he should have been awake to the evil effects of the enslavement of the negro in the American Colonies. After his return from France and while President of the Pennsylvania Assembly, a position that added to the strength of his words, he wrote and spoke often on the dangers of slavery, and aided in the formation of the Pennsylvania Society for Promoting the Abolition of Slavery and the Relief of Free Negroes Unlawfully Held in Bondage.

One address that he made on behalf of the society exhibits an almost prophetic vision of what the perils of emancipation of slaves really were. It is unnecessary to say that he was not fanatical but Franklin's expression about this is as nearly passionate as anything that he ever wrote. "Slavery is," he said, "such an atrocious debasement of human nature, that its very extirpation, if not performed with solicitous care, may sometimes open a source of serious evils." He then outlined the plans of the society for the preparation that they proposed to give freedmen for the exercise of liberty.

One thinks instinctively of Lincoln who also saw the dangers of emancipation and compares the vision of these two great souls with the wild political debauch that followed the actual emancipation of negroes in our country. The thought is not flattering to our average judgment nor to our willingness to follow the wisdom that we have.

An item in Franklin's will demonstrates that he was very much in earnest in the matter of emancipating the negro, for in it he cancels a bond of considerable size against his son-in-law in consideration of his setting free a negro slave.[7]

---

[7] "All the lands near the Ohio, and the lots near the center of Philadelphia, which I lately purchased of the State, I give to

No account of a man's religion should omit his conception of a future life. Here Franklin was entirely orthodox. He believed in the survival of personality after death and his often repeated belief did not fail him when the great adventure of death was evidently near at hand. "I look upon death," he wrote to George Whatley, "to be as necessary to our constitution as sleep. We shall rise refreshed in the morning."

There was nothing of the Spartan in his attitude nor even of resignation. He had a certain reasonable expectation that the great change was as kindly in its intent as all the other ministrations of that Providence that he had invariably believed to be dictated by a benevolent disposition toward mankind. His direct, uncomplaining, and assured attitude is seen in a letter written to Cath-

---

my son-in-law, Richard Bache, his heirs and assigns forever; I also give him the bond I have against him, of two thousand and one hundred and seventy-two pounds, five shillings, together with the interest that shall or may accrue thereon, and direct the same to be delivered up to him by my executors, canceled, requesting that, in consideration thereof, he would immediately after my decease manumit and set free his negro man Bob. I leave to him, also, the money due to me from the State of Virginia for types. . . .

> "In witness whereof, I have hereunto set my hand and seal this seventeenth day of July, in the year of our Lord one thousand and seven hundred and eighty-eight.
> "B. FRANKLIN."

erine Shipley just a year, lacking a few days, before his death. He had received her letter telling of the death of her father, the Bishop with whom Franklin had so warm a friendship. In his reply he condoled with her over the loss she had sustained and spoke of the many good qualities of her father.

Your reflections on the constant calmness and composure attending his death are very sensible. Such instances seem to show that the good sometimes enjoy in dying a foretaste of the happy state they are about to enter.

According to the course of years, I should have quitted this world long before him; I shall, however, not be long in following. I am now in my 84th year, and the last year has considerably enfeebled me, so that I hardly expect to remain another. You will then, my dear friend, consider this as probably the last line to be receiv'd from me, and as a taking leave.

Franklin's will is a beautiful document, both in its phraseology and in the high sense of responsibility that it indicates. Probably the most severe trial that he ever endured was the estrangement between his son William and himself, which was wholly of the son's choosing. William was a Tory and gave his allegiance to the British government during the Revolution and removed to England. This was a blow both to Franklin's convictions and his affections. He manifested at all times a willingness to restore the normal family relations and exhibited the grace of forgiveness in leaving to William all his lands in Nova Scotia, the books and papers in his possession, and the cancellation of all the debts of his son to himself. Furthermore, he gave to William's son, William Temple Franklin, of whom he was very fond, and who served his grandfather as his secretary while in France, three thousand acres of land in Georgia and four thousand pounds sterling.

The charity of Franklin's disposition never permitted him to cherish any grudges even against those who wronged him severely. One may search his correspondence diligently and will fail to find the note of censoriousness or bitterness anywhere. William undoubtedly hurt him more than any other person in all his life but he forgave like a father of the most magnanimous disposition.

The bulk of his property he bequeathed to his daughter Sarah and her husband, Richard Bache. Among the things that she was to receive was a picture of the king of France set with four hundred and eight diamonds, but she was requested not to "form any of those diamonds into ornaments either for herself or daughters, and thereby introduce or countenance the expensive, vain, and useless fashion of wearing jewels in this country." His years of familiarity with the French court had not succeeded in weaning him away to any false social standards.

Gratitude is said to be at once one of the finest and rarest of virtues, and we find much of it in Franklin's will. Because he had received his first instructions in literature in the free grammar schools of Boston he left one hundred pounds to those schools, the interest of which was to provide silver medals as honorary rewards for suitable scholars.

The body of the will is supplemented by a long codicil in which he stated that in a democratic state there should be no offices for profit, and that accordingly he had used the salary paid him as president of the state of Pennsylvania for gifts of large amounts to colleges, schools, and building of churches. He stipulated that the two thousand pounds still due him were to be devoted to funds of one thousand pounds each to the cities of Boston and Philadelphia. Under the management of the selectmen and the ministers of the oldest Episcopal, Congregational, and Presbyterian churches of each city the money was to be used as a loan fund to worthy artisans under twenty-five years of age to enable them to set themselves up in business. His reason for doing this was that when he was a young tradesman it was the loans of kind friends that gave him his start and laid the foundation of his fortune. At the end of each hundred years this sum, which should by that time have become over one hundred thousand pounds, was to be devoted to public improvements, excepting such amounts as were necessary to continue the loan fund.

It is interesting to know that the fund in Boston was used as directed and so nearly filled his expectations that the first centenary saw a large sum to be devoted to the city. The Philadelphia fund has not been so fortunate, but is still doing good service.

His fine crab-tree walking stick with a gold head curiously wrought in the form of the cap of liberty he left to his "friend and the friend of mankind, General Washington," and his new quarto Bible to William Hewson, the son of his dear old friend, Mrs. Mary Hewson.

And so comes to an end this incredibly varied and uniformly useful life. How any man who reads the records of his life and sentiments as mirrored in his own letters and confessions can feel that Franklin was an irreligious or unbelieving man, an agnostic or a Deist, it is hard to comprehend.

After he had weathered the storm of tumultuous doubt and adventurous thinking which had beset him in his youth he laid hold of the great spiritual realities: God, and his good disposition toward men; the duty of worship; and man's responsibility for just and kindly acts. In that faith he carried out with incredible consistency a long life blessed with prosperity in worldly goods; a prosperity that he used not for self-aggrandizement or indulgence, but for the great cause of human liberty and human betterment. It matters little that he would not subscribe to the creeds of his day; creeds that are now mostly discarded by the descendants of those who formed them; he did subscribe to the creed of Micah, "what doth the Lord require of thee but to love mercy, do justice, and to walk humbly with thy God?"

Deathbed utterances are not of any great significance unless they correspond with those made in a state of vigor, and possibly not then. The knave may die like a hero and the saint may collapse like Bunyan's Christian, crossing the dark river. Franklin's last days were of the same pattern as all the rest. His physician has left a very minute account of them. He was at intervals in very great agony but in the better moments was as cheerful and witty as ever.

Mrs. Hewson, to whose son William Franklin left his Bible, wrote to a friend:

I was the faithful witness of the closing scene, which he sustained with that calm fortitude which characterized him through life. No repining, no peevish expression, ever escaped him during a confinement of two years, in which I believe if every moment of ease could be added together, would not amount to two whole months. . . .

I never shall forget one day that I passed with our friend last summer. I found him in bed in great agony; but, when that agony abated a little, I asked if I should read to him. He said, yes; and the first book I met with was Johnson's "Lives of the Poets." I read the Life of Watts, who was favorite author with Dr. Franklin; and, instead of lulling him to sleep, it roused him to a display of the powers of his memory and his reason. He repeated several of Watts' Lyric Poems, and descanted upon their sublimity in a strain worthy of them and of their author. It is natural for us to wish that an attention to some ceremonies had accompanied that religion of the heart, which I am convinced Dr. Franklin always possessed; but let us, who feel the benefit of them, continue to practice them, without thinking lightly of that piety, which could support pain without a murmur, and meet death without terror.

The historian Parton has a description of Franklin's last hours. "To a clerical friend who witnessed one of his paroxysms and was about to retire, he said, 'O no, don't go away. These pains will soon be over. They are for my good, and besides what are the pains of a moment in comparison with the pleasures of eternity?' He had a picture of Christ on the cross placed so that he could conveniently look at it as he lay in bed. 'That,' he would say, 'is the picture of one who came into the world to teach men to love one another.' "

It had always been his belief that God took pleasure in the pleasure of his children, and that men ought to seek to enjoy life on every side so long as their pleasure harassed neither themselves nor their fellows. The approach of death was not gloomy to him. The spirit of his last days was the spirit of his last letter to George Whitefield:

That Being who gave me existence and thro' almost three-score years has been showering his favours upon me, whose very chastisements have been blessings to me; can I doubt that he loves me? And if he loves me, can I doubt that he will go on to take care of me, not only here but hereafter. This in some may seem presumption; to me it appears the best grounded hope; hope of the future, built on experience of the past.

It is a pity that there was not placed on Franklin's tomb the epitaph that he prepared for himself, which is in itself a confession of his faith:

The Body of
B. Franklin,
Printer:

Like the Cover of an old Book,
Its Contents torn out,
And stript of its Lettering and Gilding,
Lies here, Food for Worms.
But the Work shall not be wholly lost:
For it will, as he believed, appear once more,
In a new & more perfect Edition,
Corrected and amended
By the Author.

APPENDIX I

PREFACE TO "AN ABRIDGMENT OF THE BOOK OF COMMON PRAYER"

THE Editor of the following abridgment of the Liturgy of the Church of England thinks it but decent and respectful to all, more particularly to the reverend body of clergy, who adorn the Protestant religion by their good works, preaching, and example, that he should humbly offer some reason for such an undertaking. He addresses himself to the serious and discerning. He professes himself to be a Protestant of the Church of England, and holds in the highest veneration the doctrines of Jesus Christ. He is a sincere lover of social worship, deeply sensible of its usefulness to society; and he aims at doing some service to religion, by proposing such abbreviations and omissions in the forms of our Liturgy (retaining everything he thinks essential) as might, if adopted, procure a more general attendance. For, besides the differing sentiments of many pious and well-disposed persons in some speculative points, who in general have a good opinion of our Church, it has often been observed and complained of, that the Morning and Evening Service, as practiced in England and elsewhere, are so long, and filled with so many repetitions, that the continued attention suitable to so serious a duty becomes impracticable, the mind wanders, and the fervency of devotion is slackened. Also the propriety of saying the same prayer more than once in the same service is doubted, as the service is thereby lengthened without apparent necessity; our Lord having given us a short prayer as an example, and censured the heathen for thinking to be heard because of much speaking.

Moreover, many pious and devout persons, whose age or infirmities will not suffer them to remain for hours in a cold church, especially in the winter season, are obliged to forego the comfort and edification they would receive by their attendance at divine service. These, by shortening the time, would be relieved, and the younger sort, who have had some principles of religion instilled into them, and who have been educated in a belief of the necessity of adoring their Maker, would probably more frequently, as well as cheerfully, attend divine service, if they were not detained so long at any one time. Also many well-disposed tradesmen, shopkeepers, artificers, and others, whose habitations are not remote from churches, could, and would, more frequently, at least, find time to attend divine service on other than Sundays, if the prayers were reduced to a much narrower compass.

Formerly there were three services performed at different times of the day, which three services are now usually joined in one. This may suit the convenience of the person who officiates, but it is too often inconvenient and tiresome to the congregation. If this abridgment, therefore, should ever meet with acceptance, the well-disposed clergy who are laudably desirous to encourage the frequency of divine service may promote so great and good a purpose by repeating it three times on a Sunday without so much fatigue to themselves as at present. Suppose, at nine o'clock, at eleven, and at one in the evening; and by preaching no more sermons than usual of a moderate length; and thereby accommodate a greater number of people with convenient hours.

These were general reasons for wishing and proposing an abridgment. In attempting it we do not presume to dictate even to a single Christian. We are sensible there is a proper authority in the rulers of the Church for ordering such matters; and whenever the time shall come when it may be thought not unreasonable to revise our Liturgy, there is no doubt but every suitable improvement will be made, under the care and direction of so much learning, wisdom, and piety, in one body of men collected. Such a work as this must then be much better executed. In the meantime this humble performance may serve to show the practicability of shortening the service near one half, without the omission of what is essentially necessary; and we hope, moreover, that the book may be occasionally of some use to families, or private assemblies of Christians.

To give now some account of particulars. We have presumed upon this plan of abridgment to omit the First Lesson, which is taken from the Old Testament, and retain only the Second from the New Testament, which, we apprehend, is more suitable to teach the so-much-to-be-revered doctrine of Christ, and of more immediate importance to Christians; although the Old Testament is allowed by all to be an accurate and concise history, and, as such, may more properly be read at home.

We do not conceive it necessary for Christians to make use of more than one creed. Therefore, in this abridgment are omitted the Nicene Creed and that of St. Athanasius. Of the Apostles' Creed we have retained the parts that are most intelligible and most essential. And as the Father, Son, and Holy Ghost are there confessedly and avowedly a part of the belief, it does not appear necessary, after so solemn a confession, to repeat again, in the Litany, the Son and Holy Ghost, as that part of the service is otherwise very prolix.

The Psalms being a collection of odes written by different persons, it hath happened that many of them are on the same subjects and repeat the same sentiments—such as those that complain of enemies and persecutors, call upon God for protection, express a confidence therein, and thank him for it when afforded. A very great part of the book consists of repetitions of this kind, which may therefore well bear abridgment. Other parts are merely historical, repeating the mention of facts more fully narrated in the preceding books, and which, relating to the ancestors of the Jews, were more interesting to them than to us. Other parts are local, and allude to places of which we have no knowledge, and therefore do not affect us. Others are personal, relating to the particular circumstances of David or Solomon, as kings, and can therefore seldom be rehearsed with any propriety by private Christians. Others imprecate, in the most bitter terms, the vengeance of God on our adversaries, contrary to the spirit of Christianity, which commands us to love our enemies, and to pray for those that hate us and despitefully use us. For these reasons it is to be wished that the same liberty were by the governors of our Church allowed to the minister with regard to the reading Psalms, as is taken by the clerk with regard to those that are to be sung, in directing the parts that he may judge most suitable to be read at the time, from the present circumstances of the congregation, or the tenor of his sermon, by saying, "Let us read" such and such parts of the Psalms named. Until this is done our abridgment, it is hoped, will be found to contain what may be most generally proper to be joined in by an assembly of Christian people. The Psalms are still apportioned to the days of the month, as heretofore, though the several parts for each day are generally a full third shorter.

We humbly suppose the same service contained in this abridgment might properly serve for all the saints' days, fasts, and feasts, reading only the Epistle and Gospel appropriated to each day of the month.

The Communion is greatly abridged, on account of its great length; nevertheless, it is hoped and believed that all those parts are retained which are material and necessary.

Infant Baptism in Churches being performed during divine service would greatly add to the length of that service, if it were not abridged. We have ventured, therefore, to leave out the less material parts.

The Catechism, as a compendium of systematic theology, which learned divines have written folio volumes to explain, and which, therefore, it may be presumed, they thought scarce intelligible without such expositions, is, perhaps, taken altogether, not so well adapted to the capacities of children as might be wished. Only those plain answers, therefore, which express our duty towards God, and our duty towards our neighbor, are retained here. The rest is recommended to their reading and serious consideration, when more years shall have ripened their understanding.

The Confirmation is here shortened.

The Commination and all cursing of mankind is, we think, best omitted in this abridgment.

The form of solemnization of Matrimony is often abbreviated by the officiating minister at his discretion. We have selected what appears to us the material parts, and which we humbly hope will be deemed sufficient.

The long prayers in the service for the Visitation of the Sick seem not so proper, when the afflicted person is very weak and in distress.

The Order for the Burial of the Dead is very solemn and moving; nevertheless, to preserve the health and lives of the living, it appeared to us that this service ought particularly to be shortened. For numbers standing in the open air with their hats off, often in tempestuous weather, during the celebration, its great length is not only inconvenient, but may be dangerous to the attendants. We hope, therefore, that our abridgment of it will be approved by the rational and prudent.

The Thanksgiving of women after childbirth being, when read, part of the service of the day, we have also, in some measure, abridged.

Having thus stated very briefly our motives and reasons, and our manner of proceeding in the prosecution of this work, we hope to be believed, when we declare the rectitude of our intentions. We mean not to lessen or prevent the practice of religion, but to honour and promote it. We acknowledge the excellency of our present Liturgy, and, though we have shortened it, we have not presumed to alter a word in the remaining text; not even to substitute who for which in the Lord's Prayer, and elsewhere, although it would be more correct. We respect the characters of bishops and other dignitaries of our Church, and, with regard to the inferior clergy we wish that they were more equally provided for, than by that odious and vexatious as well as unjust method of gathering tithes in kind, which creates animosities and litigations, to the interruption of the good harmony and respect which might otherwise subsist between the rectors and their parishioners.

And thus, conscious of upright meaning, we submit this abridgment to the serious consideration of the prudent and dispassionate, and not to enthusiasts and bigots; being convinced in our own breasts, that this shortened method, or one of the same kind better executed, would further religion, increase unanimity, and occasion a more frequent attendance on the worship of God.

APPENDIX II

PROPOSED NEW VERSION OF THE BIBLE

To the Printer of * * *

Sir:

It is now more than one hundred and seventy years since the translation of our common English Bible. The language in that time is much changed, and the style, being obsolete, and thence less agreeable, is perhaps one reason why the reading of that excellent book is of late so much neglected. I have therefore thought it would be well to procure a new version, in which, preserving the sense, the turn of phrase and manner of expression should be modern. I do not pretend to have the necessary abilities for such a work myself; I throw out the hint for the consideration of the learned; and only venture to send you a few verses of the first chapter of Job, which may serve as a sample of the kind of version I would recommend.

A. B.

Part of the First Chapter of Job
Modernized

Old Text	*New Version*
Verse 6. Now there was a day when the sons of God came to present themselves before the Lord, and Satan came also amongst them.	Verse 6. And it being *Levee* day in heaven, all God's nobility came to court, to present themselves before him; and Satan also appeared in the circle, as one of the ministry.
7. And the Lord said unto Satan, Whence comest thou? Then Satan answered the Lord, and said, From going to and fro in the earth, and from walking up and down in it.	7. And God said to Satan, You have been some time absent; where were you? And Satan answered I have been at my country-seat, and in different places visiting my friends.
8. And the Lord said unto Satan, Hast thou considered my servant Job, that there is none like him in the earth, a perfect and an upright man, one that feareth God, and escheweth evil?	8. And God said, Well, what think you of Lord Job? You see he is my best friend, a perfectly honest man, full of respect for me, and avoiding everything that might offend me.
9. Then Satan answered the Lord, and said, Doth Job fear God for naught?	9. And Satan answered, Does your Majesty imagine that his good conduct is the effect of mere personal attachment and affection?
10. Hast thou not made an hedge about his house, and about all that he hath on every side? Thou hast blessed the work of his hands, and his substance is increased in the land.	10. Have you not protected him, and heaped your benefits upon him, till he is grown enormously rich?

11. But put forth thine hand now, and touch all that he hath, and he will curse thee to thy face.

11. Try him—only withdraw your favor, turn him out of his places, and withhold his pensions, and you will soon find him in the opposition.

[1779?]

APPENDIX III

THE LORD'S PRAYER

Old Version	*New Version by B. F.*
1. Our Father which art in Heaven,	1. Heavenly Father,
2. Hallowed be thy Name.	2. May all revere thee,
3. Thy Kingdom come.	3. And become thy dutiful Children and faithful Subjects.
4. Thy will be done on Earth as it is in Heaven.	4. May thy Laws be obeyed on Earth as perfectly as they are in Heaven.
5. Give us this Day our daily Bread.	5. Provide for us this Day as thou hast hitherto daily done.
6. Forgive us our debts as we forgive our Debtors.	6. Forgive us our Trespasses and enable us likewise to forgive those that offend us.
7. And Lead us not into Temptation, but deliver us from Evil.	7. Keep us out of Temptation, and deliver us from Evil.—

Reason for the Change of Expression

Old Version.—Our Father Which Art in Heaven.

New Version.—Heavenly Father. This is more concise, equally expressive, and better modern English.

Old Version.—Hallowed Be Thy Name. This seems to relate to an Observance among the Jews not to pronounce the proper or peculiar Name of God, they deeming it a *Proper Name* for God; the word God being a common or general Name, expressing all chief Objects of Worship, true or false. The Word *Hallowed* is almost obsolete. People now have but an imperfect Conception of the Meaning of the Petition. It is therefore proposed to change the expression into

New Version.—May all Revere Thee.

Old Version.—Thy Kingdom Come. This Petition seems suited to the then Condition of the Jewish Nation. Originally their State was a Theocracy. God was their King. Dissatisfied with that kind of Government, they desired a visible earthly King in the manner of the Nations round them. They had such Kings accordingly; but their Offerings were *due* to God on many Occasions by the Jewish Law, which when People could not pay, or had forgotten as Debtors are apt to do, it was proper to pray that those Debts might be forgiven. Our Liturgy uses neither the *debtors* of Matthew, nor the *indebted* of Luke, but instead of them speaks of *those that trespass against us*. Perhaps the Considering it as a Christian Duty to forgive Debtors, was by the Compilers thought an inconvenient Idea in a trading Nation. There seems however something presumptuous in this Mode of Expression, which has the Air of proposing ourselves as an Example of Goodness fit for God to imitate. *We hope you will at least be as good as we are;* you see we forgive one another, and therefore we pray that you would forgive us. Some have considered it in another sense, *forgive us as we forgive others;* that is, if we do not forgive others we pray that thou wouldst not forgive us. But this being a kind of conditional *imprecation* against ourselves, seems improper in such a Prayer; and therefore it may be better to say humbly & modestly

New Version.—Forgive Us Our Trespasses, and Enable Us Likewise to Forgive Those That Offend Us. This instead of assuming that we have already in & of ourselves the Grace of Forgiveness, acknowledges our Dependence on God, the Fountain of Mercy for any Share we may have in it, praying that he would communicate of it to us. . .

Old Version.—And Lead Us Not into Temptation. The Jews had a Notion, that God sometimes tempted, or directed or permitted the Tempting of People. Thus it was said he tempted Pharaoh; directed Satan to tempt Job; and a false Prophet to tempt Ahab, &c. Under this Persuasion it was natural for them to pray that he would not put them to such severe Trials. We now suppose that Temptation, so far as it is supernatural, comes from the Devil only, and this Petition continued conveys a Suspicion which in our present Conception seems unworthy of God, therefore might be altered to

New Version.—Keep Us Out of Temptation. Happiness was not increas'd by the Change, and they had reason to wish and pray for a Return of the Theocracy, or Government of God. Christians in these Times have other Ideas when they speak of the Kingdom of God, such as are perhaps more adequately express'd by

New Version.—And Become Thy Dutiful Children & Faithful Subjects.

Old Version.—Thy Will Be Done on Earth As It Is in Heaven.

New Version.—May Thy Laws Be Obeyed on Earth as Perfectly as They Are in Heaven.

Old Version.—Give us This Day Our Daily Bread. Give us what is OURS, seems to put us in a Claim of Right, and to contain too little of the grateful Acknowledgment and Sense of Dependence that becomes Creatures who live on the daily Bounty of their Creator. Therefore it is changed to

New Version.—Provide for Us This Day, As Thou Hast Hitherto Daily Done.

Old Version.—Forgive Us Our Debts As We Forgive Our Debtors. Matthew.

Forgive Us Our Sins, for We Also Forgive Every One That Is Indebted to Us. Luke.

[1778?]

(2)

THE END

DATE DUE